STEMscopes™

TEXAS

STEMscopedia – 4, English

ISBN: **978-1-63037-016-9**

To learn more, visit us at www.acceleratelearning.com

3rd Printing 2015

TABLE OF CONTENTS

reflect

Do you know what air, water, and an apple all have in common? They are all examples of matter. *Matter* is a word we use a lot in science. It means "stuff." All of the stuff in the world that has **mass** and takes up space is called matter.

An apple is a solid, water is a liquid, and the air in a balloon is a gas.

There is solid stuff like an apple. There is liquid stuff like water. There is also gas stuff like the air in a balloon. What other examples of matter can you see around you right now?

What are the properties of matter?

The matter around us has many properties. *Properties* help us to describe and compare different types of matter. Think of properties as ways of describing the things around us. Are they big or small, hot or cold, heavy or light? Here are some basic properties of matter:

- **Size:** Matter can be very big like the planet Earth or very small like a tiny piece of dust.

- **Mass:** An object can contain a lot of matter—for example, a brick. An object can contain very little matter—for example, an empty box. The brick has more mass than the empty box, even if they are the same size.

- **Volume:** Matter can take up a lot of space like the ocean or just a little space like a snowflake. The ocean has more volume than the snowflake.

- **Temperature:** Matter can be hot like lava or cold like ice. The lava has a higher temperature than the ice.

This thermometer in the picture measures the temperature of this liquid.

look out!

It is important to remember that some matter is difficult to observe. For example, we sometimes forget that air is matter because it is invisible and hard to feel. Even though we can't see air, it takes up space. When we blow into a balloon, we can watch the balloon get bigger. That's evidence we can use to show air really has mass!

CLASSIFYING MATTER

Another thing to remember is that not all solids are hard solids like a table or a brick. Some solids can be soft. Touch the clothes you are wearing right now. Are your clothes a solid, liquid, or gas? Even though something feels soft and moves around, it is still a solid.

what do you think? •

Look at the two pictures below. The picture on the left is a shadow of someone on a bike. The picture on the right is a boy riding a bike. Which of these pictures is an example of matter? Why do you think this? What is the state of matter in the picture on the right? How can you measure the shadow? How can you measure the bike?

How do we measure matter?
There are many different ways to measure matter. Let's use an apple as an example of matter. The apple can be weighed on the scale, as shown in the picture. A ruler can be used to measure the height and width of the apple. How can you measure how much space the apple takes up? Place the apple in a tub of water and watch how much the water level rises. A thermometer can be used to measure the temperature of the apple. What are other ways an apple can be measured?

How can we compare and contrast matter?
Sometimes we need to compare different types of matter. But how do we do that? We can ask a few questions to help us think about matter:

- What is the state of matter? (Is it a solid, liquid, or gas?)

- Does the matter sink or does it float? (What do we notice when we put the matter in water?)

- Is the matter magnetic? (Does the matter stick to a magnet?)

These paperclips are magnetic. They stick to the magnet.

Accelerate Learning™

try now •

Let's think about matter by comparing two everyday items.

1. Get two cans of cola: A can of diet cola and a can of regular cola. (Use the same brand of cola that are the same size. Do not open the cans of cola.)

2. Fill a large tub with water.

3. Put the regular can of cola in the water and record what you see. (Does it sink or float?)

4. Place the diet can of cola in the water and record what you see. (Does it sink or float?)

5. What did you notice about the cans of cola?

6. Why do you think there was a difference between the two cans?

Career Corner: Chemist
Chemists are scientists who study matter. These women and men think about the smallest parts of matter called *atoms* and *molecules*. Making careful measurements and closely observing their experiments is very important to chemists. Chemists understand how to combine matter in different ways and how different things react when you combine them. They make new types of matter that help us solve problems. For example, a chemist might make a new type of glue or medicine. They do this by testing different combinations of materials.

What Do You Know?
We can compare and contrast different types of matter. Use the Box and T-Chart on the next page to compare and contrast a ruler and a paperclip. How are they similar? How are they different? Make sure to include the following in your answer:

• What is the state of matter?

• Is it magnetic or not?

• Does it sink or float?

CLASSIFYING MATTER

Wood Ruler	Paperclip
How are they the same?	
How is the ruler different? Think about what happens when it is placed in water. Think about how it reacts to a magnet.	How is the paperclip different? Think about how what happens when it is placed in water. Think about how it reacts to a magnet.

Measuring the Matter Around Us

It is very important for elementary students to develop an understanding of matter. Young learners typically have an understanding of solids and liquids as matter, but they may need some support in grasping that air is also matter. Your child may also struggle to understand that "soft" solids like powder, cloth, and paper are solids.

Your child has been learning about the properties of matter. Provide them with some opportunities to measure the following properties:

- Size (Use a ruler to measure height, width, and length.)
- Mass (At this level, it is appropriate to measure weight.)
- Volume (It is easier to measure powders and liquids than solids.)
- Temperature (Use a thermometer or record whether something feels warm or cool to the touch, exercising caution not to burn yourself.)

Provide your child opportunities to measure and compare types of matter based on the properties listed above. Your child should also use the following questions to compare types of matter:

- What is the state of matter? (Is it a solid, a liquid, or a gas?)
- Is the matter magnetic? (Does the matter stick to a magnet?)
- Does the matter sink or float? (What do we notice when we put the matter in water?)

Pick some safe household objects (milk, sugar, paperclips, water, ice cubes, cloth, paper, etc.), and help your child determine the state of matter, whether the object is magnetic, and whether the object sinks or floats.

Help your child understand that all states of water—solid, liquid, and gas—are water. The water particles are the same in each state, but the way those particles move around are different depending on whether they are being heated or cooled.

Here are some questions to discuss with your child:

- How is all matter similar?
- How can we compare different types of matter?
- What are some ways to measure matter?
- Is _____ matter? (Show some examples that are not matter—such as a shadow, heat, light, love, etc.—to see if your child understands this concept.)

Accelerate Learning™

reflect

Water is one of the most important parts of our planet. All living things need water to survive. You use many forms of water every day. You may use ice (solid water) to keep your iced tea cold. You drink liquid water and use it to take baths and showers. But did you know that there is also water in the air that you cannot see? How does water get into the air? How does water in the air get back to the ground?

What happens to the outside of a glass when you pour ice water into it?
When you put ice in a glass of water, the ice cools off the water and the glass. But the ice is also cooling the air around the glass. Cooling the air causes something surprising to happen. Do you know what happens?

The air around us contains water in the form of a gas, called *water vapor*. When the ice cools the air next to the glass, the water in the air changes from a gas into liquid water. That liquid water forms drops of water on the side of the glass. These drops are called *condensation*. Cooling causes condensation to form on surfaces like mirrors and drinking glasses. So, cooling can cause water to change its physical state from a gas to a liquid. Think about when you've seen it happen—what do those drops on the glass look like?

What are some other examples of condensation? Have you ever seen drops of water on the grass in a cool morning? That's one example. Droplets on the windshield of a car in the morning are another example.

Everyday Life: Water on My Tea!
Have you ever made a glass of iced tea? Maybe you started with warm tea. You added some ice to cool it off. After a few minutes you noticed that there were drops of water on the side of the glass. There was also water in a puddle around the bottom of the glass. This is an example of condensation. Where did this water come from? The water on the side of the glass came from water that we cannot see in the air!

look out!

It is important to remember that condensation on a glass comes from water in the air around the glass. The water in the air cools and forms drops of water on the glass. Some people think that condensation comes from the water inside the glass. This is not correct.

Accelerate Learning™

CHANGES FROM HEAT

Ask your friends and family members where they think the water on the side of a cold glass comes from. Do they think it comes from the air or from the water in the glass? You may be surprised by their answers. Pass along your new knowledge! Let them know the water drops come from the air around the glass.

what do you think? •

Take a look at these pictures. The picture on the left shows ice cubes sitting in a puddle of water. The picture on the right shows a glass of iced tea with drops of water on the side. Where did the puddle of water under the ice cubes come from? Where did the drops of water on the glass come from? Support your answers with evidence: How do you know?

What happens to ice when it is heated?
Imagine that you take five ice cubes and put them on the road on a warm summer day. You let them sit for a few minutes, and then you come back. What do you think you will see? You will probably see a puddle of liquid water! But where did the ice go?

Ice is solid water. Ice has the same particles as liquid water, but they are packed together and don't move around each other the same as they do in liquid water. The particles of liquid water can flow and move around each other. That is why it is hard to hold liquid water in your hand. The particles move around each other and around your hand. Ice is easier to hold in your hand because the particles don't move around the same way.

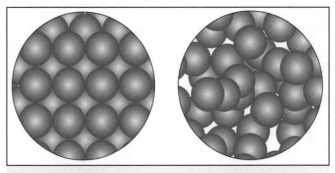

The particles in a solid (left) are packed tightly together. The particles in a liquid (right) move easily around each other, which is why we can pour liquids.

When ice is heated, the particles in the ice start to move more quickly. The water changes from a solid state (ice) to a liquid state (water). Remember that cooling causes water vapor to change to liquid water. Similarly, heating causes ice to change to liquid water.

How can we stop water from changing state?

Sometimes we don't want ice to melt quickly. We may want to use the ice to keep food or drinks cold. So we use insulating materials. *Insulating materials* help to keep objects cool or warm. These materials make it more difficult for heat to melt the ice. Can you think of some examples of things that we use to keep ice from melting? You may have a lunch box that keeps your sandwich cold or a thermos that keeps your drink cold. These materials slow heat from melting the ice. The ice in a thermos lasts longer and keeps food and drinks cold.

Scientists in the Spotlight: Adrienne Block

You know that ice is cold. Imagine being surrounded by ice and snow all day long. Polar scientist Adrienne Block doesn't work in a lab. She works in one of the coldest place on the planet: Antarctica. Block lives and works in the cold so that she can learn about mountains that are buried deep beneath thick ice sheets. Did the mountains form beneath water that later froze? Did the ice sheets slide over mountains that had already formed? Block and her team are working hard to answer these questions. How do you think insulating materials might be useful to these scientists?

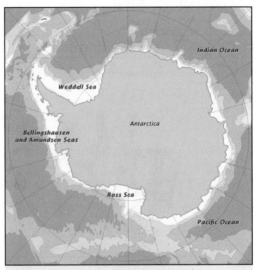

The mountains that Block is exploring are located in the center of Antarctica, about 4 km beneath the ice.

try now •

Let's take a closer look at melting ice.

1. Get two ice cubes and two plastic bags.
2. Seal one ice cube in each bag.
3. Put one bag on a table. Put the other bag in a cooler, lunch bag, or thermos.
4. Make a prediction about which ice cube will last longer.
5. Check each bag after 10 minutes and record what you see.
6. After another 10 minutes, check each bag again. Record what you see. Keep watching the ice in the bags until both cubes have melted.
7. Which ice cube melted first, the one on the table or the one in the insulated bag?
8. Why didn't the ice cubes melt at the same rate?

what do you think? •

You have seen how heating and cooling can cause an object to change state. Heating and cooling can cause other changes as well. For example, cooking cake batter in an oven causes its texture to change. The heat changes gooey, sticky batter to a moist but firm cake. Heat can also cause changes in color. Cooking a roast changes the meat from pink to reddish-brown. Can you think of other changes that result from heating or cooling?

CHANGES FROM HEAT

What Do You Know?

We see many forms of water every day. The table on the next page shows two examples. Describe the water in each picture on the next page. Explain how heating or cooling caused the changes in state.

Melting Ice		Condensation on a Spider Web	
How is the water changing?	*What causes this change?*	*How is the water changing?*	*What causes this change?*

connecting with your child •

Water Scavenger Hunt

To help your child learn more about water and how it moves and changes, lead them on a water scavenger hunt. Help them to identify all of the places in your home and surrounding area where forms of water are present. Make sure to help your child identify not only liquid water and ice (solid water), but also evidence of water vapor (water as a gas in the air). Also guide them to notice how heating and cooling can change the form of water and where insulating materials are being used (insulated lunch bag, thermos, etc).

Examples include:

- Liquid water from the sink, bathtub, or toilet

- Ice (solid water) in the freezer, a drink, or outside on a winter day

- Water that came from the air: e.g., condensation on the side of a glass of ice water, on the windshield, on the grass in the morning, etc

Help your child to understand that all forms of water—solid, liquid, and gas—are water. The water particles are the same in each form; they simply move around differently.

Here are some questions to discuss with your child:

- How are all forms of water similar?

- What are the characteristics of different forms of water?

- How does heating and cooling affect water and ice?

- What are some examples of condensation? (Examples: dew on the grass; a fogged-up windshield or bathroom mirror; drops on the outside of a glass of ice water)

reflect •

Everything around us is made out of tiny bits of **matter**. These particles may combine in different ways to produce new materials. Sometimes we need to separate the parts of a material. If we know how the small bits are combined, we can often figure out how to separate them.

> **matter:** what is commonly called "stuff"; anything that has mass and takes up space

In this lesson, we will focus on three different types of materials. Some examples include pure water, sea water, and rocky soil. How are these materials similar? How are they different?

Each of these materials is formed from different ingredients. We may separate these particles in different ways. How would you separate the parts that make up each material? How you plan to separate the parts will tell you more about the type of material.

How is seawater different from pure water? How is it different from rocky soil?

What is a mixture?

First we must learn the difference between *mixtures* and *compounds*. Sometimes particles combine to form a completely new kind of material. The particles become connected in new ways that are difficult to undo. In these cases, we say a *compound* has formed.

Other times, particles do not form a new material when they combine. The connections between the particles are not difficult to undo. In these cases, we say a *mixture* has formed.

Rocky road ice cream is a mixture. Combining marshmallows, almonds, and chocolate ice cream does not create a new kind of material.

Making a mixture does not create a new material. This is true even when the mixture looks very different from the particles combined to make it. Compared to compounds, mixtures can be unmixed pretty easily. Later in this lesson, you will learn how. How you decide to "un-mix" something reveals whether something is a true mixture.

Accelerate Learning™

13

MIXTURES

try now •

You will need some marbles, a shoebox, and something that can cut holes in the shoebox. Cut several round holes in the bottom of the box. Make the holes a little bigger than the marbles. Cut several squares out of the lid. The squares should be as wide as the marbles. The bottom of the box, the marbles, and the squares should look like this:

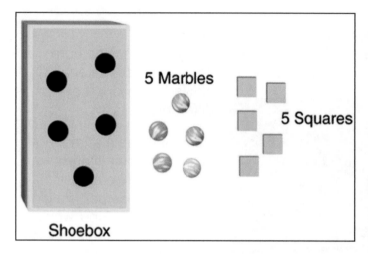

5 Marbles

5 Squares

Shoebox

Put the marbles and the squares into the shoe box, creating a mixture. Then, shake the box back and forth. How will this help you to separate the marbles from the squares? What properties of the two shapes allow you to separate them?

Imagine adding a cup of cooking oil to a cup of water in a bottle. You screw the cap onto the bottle and shake the bottle. Now the liquid looks cloudy. Is this a mixture? When you let the bottle sit still for ten minutes, the oil rises to the top. Now you see a layer of water on the bottom and a layer of oil on top. But is this a mixture?

What is a solution?

We saw that materials can be either compounds or mixtures. However, scientists identify two different kinds of mixtures. The mixture of marbles and squares in the "Try This" activity is one kind of mixture. In this kind of mixture, you can still see the bits of the materials that make up the mixture. The bits haven't changed. They still look the same as they did at the beginning before you shook them up.

The ocean is a solution of salt dissolved in water.

Accelerate Learning™

Picture what happens when you mix salt with water. What about mixing sugar with water? The salt and sugar seem to disappear into the water. How is that possible? Things don't just disappear. The answer is that salt water and sugar water are examples of a different type of mixture called *solutions*. In a solution, the parts are mixed all the way down to the smallest particles. These particles are much too small to see, but they are still there. They haven't changed. Compared to the other kind of mixture, the parts in a solution are much more evenly and randomly mixed.

When materials like salt and sugar "disappear" into a liquid, we say they have *dissolved*. Later we will see how dissolved materials can be made to reappear. Solutions are separated in a different way from other mixtures.

Remember, mixtures and solutions are not separate things. A solution is one *kind* of mixture. All solutions are mixtures, but not all mixtures are solutions.

look out!

When ice melts, it changes to water. Sugar and salt can also melt if they get very hot. When they do, they become clear like water. When sugar and salt dissolve, they form clear solutions. Does this mean that melting is the same as dissolving?

Not at all! Melting is what is called a *change of state*. Solid, liquid, and gas are three different states of matter. Melting is a change from a solid state to a liquid state. Melting does not form a solution because only one material is there. Salt water and sugar water are mixtures because two materials are being mixed. Just because everything ends up as a liquid does not mean that anything has melted.

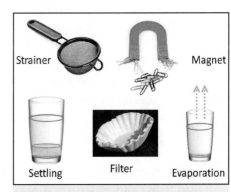

Mixtures can be separated in different ways.

How can materials in a mixture or solution be separated?

If a material is a mixture, it can be separated by *physical processes*. If a process is physical, it does not involve creating any new materials. For example, you can separate a mixture of sand and rocks with a strainer. The sand will fall through the holes, and the rocks will stay in the strainer.

A strainer wouldn't separate a mixture of sawdust and sand because sawdust particles and sand particles are about the same size. To separate this mixture, you could dump it into a bucket of water. The sand would sink and

These piles of salt were produced by letting ocean water evaporate.

the sawdust would float. Now think about sand mixed in water. How could you separate those items? Perhaps you could use a filter. A filter can separate a mixture of small bits like sand in a liquid. The paper in a filter has very small holes that let water pass through but not solid particles like sand. How about metal items? There are tools that can help us separate those items, too. A magnet can help us separate some types of mixtures. Magnets attract anything made of iron. You could use a magnet to separate pins from toothpicks.

What happens when water or a water solution is exposed to air? (A water solution is water with something dissolved in it.) Water molecules leave the liquid and move into the air as a gas. This process is called *evaporation*. As water evaporates, the dissolved material is left behind.

Solutions are usually separated by evaporation. Warming the liquid speeds up the evaporation process. If a solution of salt water or sugar water were allowed to completely evaporate, the salt or sugar would be visible at the bottom of the container. The salt and sugar particles would look much as they did before they were dissolved.

All the processes mentioned above are physical processes. The other kind of process is a *chemical* process. In a chemical process, a new material is formed. For example, hydrogen and oxygen are two pure gases that combine to form water. The water is not a mixture. It is a new material that is different from the beginning ingredients. The water can be separated into hydrogen and oxygen, but not by any physical process.

Looking to the Future: Drinking the Ocean

"Water, water, everywhere, nor any drop to drink." This is a line from a famous poem about sailors on a ship in the middle of the ocean who run out of water to drink. The sailors are surrounded by water, but they can't drink it because ocean water is salt water.

More and more people have a problem just like the sailors. Fresh water on Earth is running out. Some countries near the ocean have started to separate ocean water into salt and pure water to drink and water their crops. Separating salt from seawater is called *desalination*. We already learned that this can be done by evaporation. But we don't need to lose the evaporated water to the air. It can be recaptured as liquid water.

When you desalinate seawater using evaporation, you need a lot of heat. Producing heat is expensive. Most desalination happens in countries that have three things in common: They don't get much rain, they are near the ocean, and they have a lot of fuel to make heat.

It is important to find better, cheaper ways to desalinate water if we are going to solve Earth's fresh water shortage. Scientists are working hard to make evaporation cheaper and to find ways other than evaporation to remove salt from seawater.

what do you think? •

Why is the ocean salty but rivers are not? Think about how water moves on Earth. The land contains many compounds, including salts. Rivers run over land to the sea. Water evaporates into the air where it forms clouds. Rain falls from the clouds and runs into the rivers.

What Do You Know?
A mixture contains these parts:

- Sand
- Sawdust
- Iron pieces
- Salt
- Glass marbles

Below are six steps in a process that can separate all the parts of this mixture. Put the steps in the correct order. Write a 1 in front of the first step, a 2 in front of the second step, and so forth. Also, write the part that will be separated as a result of each step. A few of the steps can happen at different times.

Order	Step	What part will it separate?
	Pour the mixture into a bucket of water.	
	Pass a magnet through the mixture.	
	Pass the mixture through a screen.	
	Evaporate the water.	
	Pour the mixture through a filter.	
	Remove material floating on the surface.	

MIXTURES

Separating Mixtures by Evaporation

A solution is also called a *homogeneous mixture*. This means that the parts are thoroughly mixed and we don't usually see the separate parts easily. For example, when sugar dissolves in water, individual sugar particles separate from the larger sugar grains and become surrounded by water particles. Salt water is also a homogeneous mixture. The other type of mixture is a *heterogeneous mixture*. In this case, the individual bits of the components are larger than the small particles, as in a mixture of salt and sand. As a result, the ingredients are more clumped, or less random.

Solutions (homogeneous mixtures) are most easily separated by evaporation. This process allows the solvent (for example, water) to leave the solution and enter the atmosphere as gas molecules (for example, water vapor). This is how evaporation happens: In both pure water and in a water solution, particles of water are always passing back and forth between the liquid and the air at the surface. Evaporation happens when more molecules leave the solution than enter. Heat and surface area both increase the rate of evaporation. In the case of a solution, evaporation eventually leads to the loss of all the water, leaving behind the original dissolved material as a solid. This solid will be little changed from its original form before it was dissolved.

You can perform this activity with your child to observe the dissolution and recovery by evaporation of salt and sugar from a solution. Follow these steps:

1. Measure a sample of sugar and a sample of salt of equal size. If a scale or balance is available, make the samples of equal mass.

2. Add identical volumes of water to identical glasses.

3. Add the sugar sample to one glass and the salt sample to the other glass, and stir until dissolved. Observe any difference in the rate of dissolution.

4. Pour each solution into identical pie pans or other wide-mouth containers. Do not keep track of which is which.

5. Put the samples in a place where they are safe from contamination.

6. When all the water has evaporated, find the mass of the solids.

7. Ask your child to identify the samples. Which is the sugar, and which is the salt?

Here are some questions to discuss with your child:

1. Did the salt and sugar change in any way during the experiment?

2. Did a chemical change take place? Why or why not?

3. What physical changes occurred?

4. Can evaporation be used to separate a mixture of salt and sugar?

reflect •

It's 3 p.m., and your friends are doing different things. Jake is kicking a soccer ball while he's at soccer practice. His friend Tyler is melting butter in a pot to make macaroni and cheese while he's at home. Christina just turned on her laptop to play a computer game. She can hear Shannon next door, playing the piano.

All of these activities require energy. However, each kid is using a different kind of energy. Do you know what types of energy they are using?

Jake is using *mechanical energy* to run and kick the ball. Tyler's snack requires *heat energy* to cook the food. Christina uses *light energy* and *electrical energy* to see and run her computer game. She can hear Shannon playing the piano because of *sound energy*. We use all five forms of energy for almost everything we do.

What type of energy is used in each of these photos?

FORMS OF ENERGY

What are different forms of energy?

Are you full of energy? Actually you are, even if you're sleeping. Energy is keeping your body warm. It takes energy to close your eyes and yawn. We are surrounded by energy—in the air, under our feet, in our bodies. We use it every day in all of its forms. *Energy* is the ability to do work. It is the power to cause change. Let's explore some of the different forms of energy.

- **Mechanical Energy:** Anything that moves is using mechanical energy. When you play soccer, you are using mechanical energy to kick the ball. Cats use mechanical energy to stretch, and ants use it to carry away crumbs. Even things that are not alive can generate mechanical energy. A car uses mechanical energy to move people across town.

what do you think? •

How are water and air producing mechanical energy in these photos?

- **Heat and Thermal Energy:** When your heart is racing and your body is sweating, you know that you are using energy. The heat that your body gives off by sweating is also energy. We know this because everything is made up of tiny particles. These particles are always moving. Even in a frozen solid like ice, the particles are moving very slowly. The total energy of these moving particles is called *thermal energy*. *Heat* is a form of energy that causes these particles to move faster. Think about adding heat to a pot of water on the stove. It gets hotter, right? This means that its temperature increases.

look out! •

Just because an object heats up does not mean the object will stay hot. Notice how bath water starts to cool as you sit in it. The water is hot because its particles are moving very quickly. It has a lot of thermal energy. However, the air particles over the water absorb the water's heat. Over time, the water particles slow down, and the bath water cools.

- **Light Energy:** The Sun keeps us warm. It also provides another type of energy that we use every day—*light energy*. Light travels in a straight line from the point where it starts. It can pass through a clear piece of glass or plastic. However, if it hits a solid object that you cannot see through, it will bend. Another term used to describe light bending is *refraction.*

Shadows are created when light is stopped from going farther. A shiny object will *reflect* light. This means the light will bounce back to whomever is looking at it. You can see yourself in a mirror because it reflects light. Light energy comes from a few natural sources besides the Sun, such as fire and lightning.

try now •

Here is a fun way to see how light refracts.

1. Choose a partner.
2. Each of you can choose four different small objects around the classroom. Do not show these objects to your partner.
3. Close all the curtains.
4. Turn off the light.
5. Take turns holding up one of your objects and shining a flashlight on it.
6. Take turns guessing the objects ONLY from the shadows they cast on the wall.
7. Describe the shadow.
8. Look at the actual object. Were you right?
9. Try forming images in front of the flashlight using your fingers. You can create a whole story using finger puppets.

- **Sound Energy:** *Sound* is another type of energy we use every day. Like light, sound travels in waves. Unlike light, sound can be created by many kinds of objects. When an object vibrates, it moves nearby particles of air back and forth. These particles cause other particles to vibrate. In this way, sound waves travel through the air. If sound waves reach our ears, our brain can translate them into sound because there are small bones in our ears that vibrate. Sound requires a substance to move through, such as air or liquid. That's why sounds cannot be heard in empty space. There aren't enough particles there!

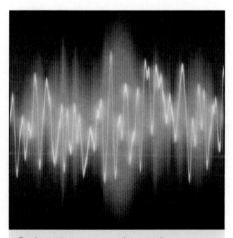

Scientists can show the sound waves that a noise creates with a sound-level meter and a computer.

Accelerate Learning™

FORMS OF ENERGY

- **Electrical Energy:** People can create both sound and light energy using another kind of energy called *electrical energy*. Remember that everything is made up of particles. Some of these particles have electrical charges. When charged particles flow along a path, they form a circuit as electrical energy. Another term for electrical energy is *electricity*.

How are forms of energy similar and different?

Scientists are able to learn about many things by observing them. We can observe some forms of energy such as light. Other forms of energy are more difficult to observe. However, scientists can still learn about these forms by observing their causes and effects. We have reviewed five forms of energy that affect us every day. They are mechanical, light, heat, sound, and electrical energy. What do these forms of energy have in common?

Each form of energy causes change or does work. For example, what happens when we put a pan of cake batter into a hot oven? Heat energy in the oven causes the particles in the batter to vibrate faster. As the temperature in the oven rises, the batter changes to a cake.

How else are these forms of energy similar? Living creatures rely on them to survive. For example, plants cannot grow without light. Plants use the energy in sunlight to make their food. People cannot survive without plants. We eat plants every day. We also feed plants to animals that help us do work or provide us with food.

Everyday Life: How do everyday objects produce or use energy?

You experience heat and thermal energy every day. Coats, scarves, and gloves keep your body warm. The furnace heats your home in the winter. The washing machine uses hot water to wash clothes. You also use hot water to take baths and showers. Your body, the air, and the water all have thermal energy.

Every movement we make needs mechanical energy. But we have also created tools and machines that help us use mechanical energy more *efficiently*, or better than we could before. Hoes, spades, and shovels help us move dirt in our own gardens. Farmers rely on huge machines such as tractors and combines to grow acres of food. They are still using mechanical energy. Cars and trains also use mechanical energy to move people quickly from one place to another.

Sound energy is our main way to communicate. We have invented many machines to help us communicate. Telephones allow people to talk over long distances. Loudspeakers broadcast our messages so people far away can hear them. Earphones let us hear music without bothering people around us. We use sounds such as sirens and whistles as warnings.

Flashing lights on a police car can be a warning. Light energy is important in our everyday activities. We must be able to see to do most of our work. So, light is now built into many of our machines. Controls in stereos, microwaves, and MP3 players all appear in light. Light bulbs allow us to make night as bright as day. Our homes have light in every room.

Most of our machines use a few different types of energy to work. Electrical energy often supplies the power to produce other kinds of energy. For example, light bulbs require electrical energy to produce light energy and a small amount of heat energy. Toasters require electrical energy to produce heat energy and a small amount of light energy. Electrical energy powers a fan, creating mechanical energy that keeps us cool.

Television is a perfect example of an invention that involves all forms of energy. It runs on electricity, which lights up a screen. The images on the screen produce sound energy. Mechanical energy is necessary to operate the controls. Also, a television produces a small amount of heat energy while operating. Can you think of other things in your home that might use many different forms of energy?

FORMS OF ENERGY

What Do You Know?

Machines help us with work we do every day. Identify the types of energy used by the machines in each photograph. Write your answers in the spaces beneath each photograph.

Play a Unique Game of 20 Questions

Road trips provide excellent teaching opportunities. While driving, play a game of 20 Questions with a twist. Choose an object that you see on the road. The other players have 20 "yes" or "no" questions to guess the object. Usually for 20 Questions, the game master tells the other players if the object is an animal, vegetable, or mineral. In this version of the game, tell the other players if the object uses or produces mechanical, thermal, light, electrical, or sound energy, or a combination of these forms. The players will need to ask questions relevant to the energy forms to guess the object correctly.

For example, you might pass cows as you are driving past a field. You would tell your child, "The thing I see uses mechanical energy, produces heat and sound energy, and sees light energy, but it neither produces nor uses electrical energy."

Here are some questions to discuss with your child:

- Does everything have some form of energy?
- If there is energy all around us, why do world leaders worry about running out of energy?
- What is renewable energy?

ELECTRICITY, CONDUCTORS AND INSULATORS

reflect ·

Imagine you want to make pasta for dinner. How do we do it? We put water in a pan and put the pan on a stove. Soon the heat from the stove burner makes the water hot enough to boil. The handle of the pan also gets hot, but the handle is not as hot as the rest of the pan. How did the heat move from the burner to the pan but not as much to the handle?

Next, you decide to turn on a flashlight to look in a dark corner in the kitchen cabinet. But how does the flashlight give off light? Energy moves through a wire from the battery to the light bulb. The energy causes the bulb to give off light. But how does energy move from one part of the flashlight to the other?

To answer these questions, we will look at what is happening inside the pan and inside the wire. We will have to imagine we can see what is happening to the particles in the pan and in the wire. Imagine zooming in to see what's really happening on a small scale.

What is a conductor?
Energy passes through some materials easily. These materials are called *conductors*. Conducted energy can be in the form of heat or electricity. To understand how heat and electricity move, we must understand that all **matter** is made up of tiny bits called *particles*.

> **matter:** the stuff that everything is made of

These particles are always moving. *Heat* is the energy of these particles when they move. If the particles in an object move faster, the object feels hotter. Picture a pot that is put on a hot stove. The particles closest to the stove burner begin to move faster and faster. Faster particles bump into slower particles nearby and cause them to speed up. This is how heat spreads. We call this spreading *conduction*.

Metals are good conductors of heat.

Solids usually conduct heat better than liquids and gases. This is because the particles in solids are closer together. Think of having a conversation with your friends—it's easier to hear them when you're closer to them, right? Particles can "communicate" with each other, too. If they're closer together, it happens more easily.

The best conductors are metals. Silver, copper, gold, aluminum, and iron are some of the best conductors of heat. Silver and gold are very expensive. This is why most pots and pans are made out of copper, aluminum, and iron. Metals are also good conductors of electricity. Lamps, toasters, TVs, and other electrical devices are connected to electrical cords.

· ·

Accelerate Learning™

ELECTRICITY, CONDUCTORS AND INSULATORS

Inside electrical cords are metal wires usually made of copper. A cord plugs into a wall socket. Inside the wall are more wires connected to electric power lines. Power lines lead to power plants that may be hundreds of miles away. Electricity is conducted from the power plant to a lamp in your home in less than a second.

look out!

What does *heat flow* mean? People used to think heat was an invisible material that flowed from hot things to cold things. That is incorrect. Heat does not flow like a river. Heat is energy, not matter. When something loses heat, it does not lose mass.

What is an insulator?
A material that is a poor conductor of energy is an insulator. Heat moves slowly through materials like glass, wood, and rubber. So, these materials are called heat insulators.

This is fiberglass insulation inside the wall of a home.

Heat also moves slowly through air and other gases. That is because the particles in these gases are far apart. Energy does not move easily from one particle to another. You might think this isn't useful, but in fact that property is very useful around our homes! Many good insulators are filled with little pockets of air. For example, the walls and ceilings of many homes are filled with fiberglass insulation. This material is made of tiny pieces of glass. The fibers form a tangled mat with many air spaces. Your house can stay a different temperature than outside because of this insulation. Can you think of other places that use insulation?

Like all animals living in cold climates, this arctic fox is well insulated by its thick fur.

Winter coats are also insulators. They prevent heat from being conducted away from our body. Many winter coats are made from fluffy materials like wool or feathers. Down clothing is a very good insulator because it has a layer of small goose feathers. Heat does not move easily through the feathers.

Electrical insulators prevent the movement of electrical energy. Earlier you read about electrical cords and wires. A layer of insulation always covers the copper wires that conduct electricity. This insulating layer is usually made of plastic, but it may also be made of rubber or cloth. These coverings keep electrical energy from moving where it shouldn't when it flows to other conductors. Insulation also makes electrical cords safe to touch.

Accelerate Learning™

ELECTRICITY, CONDUCTORS AND INSULATORS

Wood, glass, and pottery are all good electrical insulators. Pure water is an insulator, but salt water is a conductor. Tap water is also a conductor. That is because most of the water on Earth isn't pure—it contains dissolved minerals. That is why you should always be careful not to operate electrical devices around water.

what do you think? •

We often describe winter coats as warm. Or we say that a thick sweater "keeps out the cold." Are these descriptions correct? (Remember that heat is the movement of energy. So heat moves, not cold.)

try now •

Iron is a heat conductor, and wood is a heat insulator. You can see this is true by letting an iron hammer with a wooden handle lie in the sun on a hot day. After about 30 minutes, pick up the hammer. The iron head will feel much hotter than the wooden handle. Be careful not to burn yourself when you touch the iron parts, though!

The iron head feels hotter, but is it really hotter? The head and handle are actually the same temperature. Iron is a better conductor than wood. So, the heat moves to your hand faster through the iron head.

What is a circuit?

Take a look at the plug on the end of an electrical cord. Notice that it has at least two metal prongs. One prong is part of a wire that brings energy to the electrical device. The other prong is connected to a wire that carries energy away. For electricity to be useful, it must always travel in a complete, unbroken circle. That circle is called an *electrical circuit*.

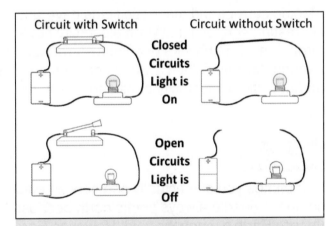

A closed electrical path completes an electrical circuit.

A circuit has several basic parts. It has a source of electrical power and something that uses electrical power. It also has wires to connect the source to the device. Most circuits also include a switch. The switch controls whether the circuit is open or closed. Broken wires or bad connections can also cause an open circuit.

Every electrical device in your home is part of such a circuit. The power source is usually an electrical power plant or a battery. A *battery* stores chemical energy that is released as electrical energy.

ELECTRICITY, CONDUCTORS AND INSULATORS

Getting Technical: Lightning Rods

A lightning strike happens when electrical energy that has built up in a cloud suddenly passes between the air and the ground. Electrical energy takes the shortest path between two points. This means one end of the lightning bolt will be the highest point on the ground. If the high point is a building, the lightening strike could set the building on fire.

In case of a lightning strike, a lightning rod conducts electricity away from a building.

Buildings that might be struck by lightning are protected by copper lightning rods. These rods are connected to the ground by thick copper wires. If lightning strikes the building, the energy will be conducted through the wire, away from the building, and into the ground. This protects the rest of the building from that energy.

How can we create an electromagnetic field?

You may know about magnets and magnetic force. A *magnet* is surrounded by invisible *lines of force* that form what is called a *magnetic field*. Magnets and objects made of iron are pushed or pulled by magnetic force when they enter a magnetic field.

Electric current and magnetic fields have an interesting connection. When electricity flows through a wire, the wire becomes surrounded by a magnetic field. When a wire is moved through a magnetic field, electricity begins to flow in the wire.

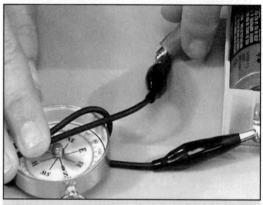

Hold the compass near the wire as you complete the circuit.

try now •

Sometimes you can actually see how an electric current creates a magnetic field. A compass needle always points north because the magnetic needle in the compass lines up with Earth's magnetic field. However, Earth's magnetic field is weak. Almost any other magnetic field will make the needle swing away from north. Think about moving a magnet near a compass—the needle will move! That means that the little magnet you have in your hand is affecting the compass more than Earth's magnetic field.

Accelerate Learning™

ELECTRICITY, CONDUCTORS AND INSULATORS

You will need a compass and something that produces an electric current. This could be as simple as a battery and a wire, as shown in the picture. Separated wires will work better than a double wire. Place the magnet near the wire, and connect one end of the wire to the battery. Observe any movement of the compass needle when the circuit is completed.

What Do You Know?

The diagram shows one or more complete circuits. It also shows one or more incomplete circuits. The diagram also includes four light bulbs. Draw a circle around the bulbs that will light up when electric current flows from the battery.

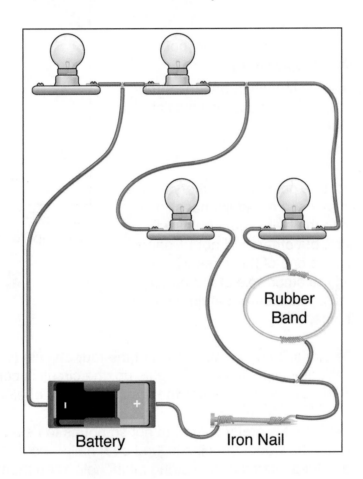

ELECTRICITY, CONDUCTORS AND INSULATORS

Conductors and Insulators

In this activity, you and your child will study electrical and thermal conductivity of four common materials: wood, plastic, aluminum, and iron. You will need:

- a piece of wood about 6 inches long, such as a chopstick, dowel, or stick

- a plastic knife

- a long aluminum nail and a long iron nail (both available at a building supply store)

- a circuit that includes a light bulb, a battery, three wires, and at least two alligator clips (all available at a typical hardware store)

- a cup that can hold hot water

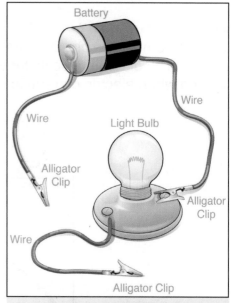

Set up your circuit like this. Attempt to complete the circuit using different objects.

Use one wire to connect one pole of the battery to one side of the bulb. (You may need an additional alligator clip to connect the wire to the bulb; some bulbs will connect directly to a wire, but others will not.) Connect the other side of the bulb to one of the wires with a clip at the end. Connect the other pole of the battery to another wire with a clip. The diagram at right shows how to put your circuit together.

Attempt to complete the circuit by connecting each of the four objects (wood, plastic, aluminum, iron) to the alligator clips. If the bulb lights up, the circuit is complete. When you are finished, take apart the circuit and discuss the results in terms of electrical conductivity.

Next, fill the cup with water that is pretty warm but not so hot as to risk a burn. Put all four of the objects into the water—the wood, the plastic, and both nails—so that each is only about half submerged. Hanging these items from a string might help keep them all halfway out of the water. After a few seconds, touch a finger to the tops of each object and compare their relative temperatures. Repeat the observation several times over the course of a minute or two. Discuss the results in terms of thermal conductivity.

Compare the electrical conductivity to the thermal conductivity for the four materials. Draw conclusions, and suggest explanations for the experimental results.

reflect

A mother hears a loud crash in the living room. She walks into the room to see her seven-year-old son looking at a broken vase on the floor.

"How did that happen?" she asks.

"I don't know. The vase just fell all by itself," the boy says.

The mother says, "It couldn't have moved by itself! Didn't you learn in school that nothing moves without a push or a pull?"

Is what the boy says possible? Or is his mother correct? In the following lesson, you will answer these and other questions about how pushes and pulls change motion.

What are some forces that can affect objects?

A *force* is a push or a pull. There are several kinds of force. Some forces are hard to notice. Other forces put on quite a show and are easy to notice! Some forces need to touch the thing they act on. Other forces can change a thing without touching it.

When someone pushes or pulls on something, it is easy to see the effect. You push on a bicycle pedal, and the bicycle moves forward. A dentist pulls on a tooth, and the tooth comes out of the patient's mouth. Other forces may seem more mysterious.

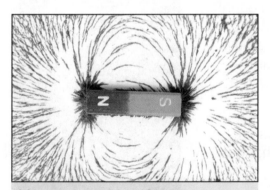

You can use bits of iron to see the field lines that surround a magnet.

For example, a *magnet* can both push and pull on another magnet. A magnet can also pull on something made of iron. This happens because of invisible lines of force surrounding the magnet. Sound impossible? Remember that even if we can't see the force, like in a magnet, it's still there!

Gravity is another force that may seem difficult to figure out. Gravity is a force that pulls all things with **mass** toward all

> **mass:** the amount of matter, or "stuff," in something

other things with mass. However, gravity is a very weak force unless one of the objects is very big, like the planet Earth. Things fall to Earth because the force of gravity pulls on them. Gravity also holds things on Earth's surface. If it weren't for gravity, things would just float away into space. Gravity is always a pull, never a push.

Accelerate Learning™

EXPERIMENTING WITH FORCES

Friction is a force that slows moving things down. Friction acts in the direction opposite to motion. Friction can also keep things from sliding around. The materials involved help make this happen. The force of friction is greater when a surface is rougher. You can walk up a steep sidewalk because friction keeps your shoes from slipping. You might not be able to walk up the same sidewalk if it were covered with ice. That is because the force of friction is much less between your shoes and the smooth ice.

what do you think? •

A car is parked on a steep street. The car is not moving. When something is not moving, we know the forces are *balanced.* This means they cancel each other out. Which force is pulling the car down the hill? Which force is balancing this force and keeping the car from sliding? (Hint: We talked about both of these forces above.)

The wall pushes back on the people. So, the forces on the wall are balanced.

What are some ways that forces affect objects?
Even pushes and pulls are not totally simple. For example, forces always come in pairs. If you push on a large tree, nothing happens. If you try to pull the tree out of the ground, nothing happens. When you push the tree, another force is balancing your push. When you pull the tree, another force is balancing your pull. But where are these other forces coming from?

When you push on a tree, the tree pushes back with an equal force. The result is that the forces are balanced and nothing moves. Similarly, when you pull on that big tree, the tree pulls back. This happens for all forces. When the force of Earth's gravity pulls you to the ground, the ground pushes up with a force equal to your weight.

Because of the force of gravity, the water speeds up as it falls.

Forces are not always balanced, however. When forces are *unbalanced*, something must change. These are the changes that can result from unbalanced forces:

• Something speeds up.

• Something slows down.

• Something changes the direction of its motion.

• Something changes shape.

These changes happen only while the force is acting. Also while the force is acting, the change keeps increasing. For example, something will keep going faster if the force keeps acting on it. When a rock is falling, the force of gravity is acting on it. Because this force is always acting on the rock, the rock goes faster and faster until it hits the ground.

• •

Accelerate Learning™

EXPERIMENTING WITH FORCES

When you throw a ball it speeds up until it leaves your hand. At that point, the force of your hand has no more effect on the ball, and the ball slows down. It slows down because of the force of friction between the air and the ball acts in the opposite direction of its motion.

try now •

You may not have realized that force is necessary to make something change direction. To see an example, first take the front wheel off of a small bicycle. If you do not already know how to do this, ask an adult for help.

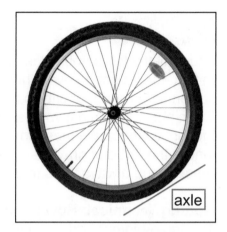

In the center of the wheel is a short axle. Hold the two ends of the axle tightly in each hand so the wheel is straight up and down. Ask someone to give the wheel a fast spin. Now, try to tilt the axle so the whole wheel tilts. You are in for a surprise. It will be very difficult to tilt the wheel because you are changing the direction of motion of something that is quite heavy. This takes more force than you may have expected.

axle

How can we test the effects of forces on an object?
Here is a simple way to study the forces of gravity, friction, and magnetism and to observe balanced and unbalanced forces. This is what you will need:

For this activity, you will need a large iron washer.

- a smooth board about 1 meter long

- a large washer made of iron

- a meter stick

- a magnet

- a sheet of sandpaper

This activity will be easier if you work with a partner. Follow these steps:

1. Put the washer at one end of the board.

2. Slowly, lift the end of the board with the washer until the washer begins to slide. Your partner should use the meter stick to measure the height of the board at the point where the washer began to slide.

3. Lower the board. Tape the magnet to one end of the board, and let the washer stick to the magnet.

4. Repeat Step 2. (If the washer can't break free from the magnet, tape a piece of cardboard to the surface of the magnet.

5. Lower the board. Remove the magnet and tape the sandpaper to one end of the board. Place the washer on the sandpaper.

6. Repeat Step 2.

Accelerate Learning™

EXPERIMENTING WITH FORCES

Based on your observations, answer these questions:

- Which forces were acting in Steps 2, 4, and 6?
- Which force was strongest: friction, magnetism, or gravity?
- Why did the washer speed up as it slid down the board?

look out! •

You may think if an object is motionless, no forces are acting on it. In fact, forces act on everything on Earth. Even when you are sitting still on the ground, gravity is pulling you toward Earth. The force of Earth pushing against you balances the force of gravity. You are motionless because these forces balance each other. It is easy to ignore the force of gravity—unless we are falling! But it is always present and always the same.

Getting Technical: How do scales work?

The force of your body pushing down on Earth's surface is called your *weight*. In America, weight is usually measured in pounds on a scale. Many scales measure weight by pushing or pulling on springs. The spring moves a pointer up or down. The number the pointer points to is the object's weight.

You may have a bathroom scale that measures weight by *compressing*—or pushing—a spring. It is easier to understand spring scales by studying a simpler scale that stretches, or pulls on, a spring. You can see these scales at most grocery stores. There is usually one hanging near the fruits and vegetables.

Try weighing different things on a spring scale. Notice that when you double the weight, the spring stretches twice as far. Two apples should weigh about twice as much as one. A quart of milk should weight about twice as much as a pint. Which force are you noticing that causes these changes?

Here is a simple spring scale. When an object hangs from the hook, it stretches a spring that moves a pointer. The pointer shows the object's weight.

reflect •

Think back to the broken vase at the beginning of this lesson. Do you think the boy broke the vase? If he did, what forces could have been involved? If he didn't, what forces could have been involved? What one force must have been involved, no matter what happened?

Accelerate Learning™

EXPERIMENTING WITH FORCES

What Do You Know?
Match the names of the forces to their descriptions. Draw a line from each force to the correct description.

gravity   slows down moving objects

spring force   pulls on iron objects

friction   used to measure weight on scales

magnetic force   makes a ball fall to the ground

Accelerate
Learning™

EXPERIMENTING WITH FORCES

Studying a Pendulum

You can use a simple pendulum to study the forces of gravity and friction with your child. You can quickly make a pendulum with a weight (called a bob), a string, and a point to hang it from, as shown in the following diagram.

Gravity is the force that always returns the bob from the height of its swing to the bottom of the arc, and friction is the force that gradually slows the pendulum down. Sources of friction are air resistance and mechanical friction at the pivot point. (In other words, the pendulum rubs against the point around which it swings. As it rubs, some of its energy changes to heat and is lost from the system.)

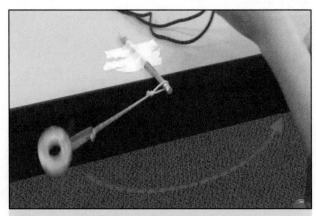

To make a simple pendulum, tape a pencil to a desk so one end of the pencil hangs over the edge of the desk. Tie one end of a string to the pencil and the other end to an iron washer (the bob). Raise the bob so it is level with the desk; then, release the bob and watch your pendulum swing.

You can also introduce your student to kinetic and potential energy. Explain how potential energy (PE) is at a maximum at the top of the pendulum's arc and that this energy is converted to kinetic energy (KE) as the bob falls to the bottom of the arc.

Studying how the variables of the pendulum affect the period of its motion is interesting. The *period* is the length of time it takes the bob to travel from one high point to the other high point. The variables are the mass of the bob, the length of the string, and the height from which the bob is dropped. You may not have expected this, but only the length of the string affects the period. Try changing each of the variables separately as you measure the period. Measuring the time it takes to make many swings and then dividing by the number of swings will give you the most accurate information.

Here are some questions to discuss with your child:

1. Was the force of friction acting on the pendulum very strong? How can you tell?
2. Name three places you have seen pendulum motion.
3. Which things affect the period of a pendulum?
4. If you replaced the metal bob with a playing card, how would the motion of the pendulum change and why?

Accelerate Learning™

reflect •

You and your family are taking a vacation and are driving a long way. You drive through a few different states along the way. When you stop in the first state, you observe that the soil is dark and rocky. In the next state, you find reddish, smooth soil. A few hours later, you stop in a state that has sandy, rough soil.

Earth has many types of soil. *Soil* contains broken-up, or *weathered*, rocks. It also contains broken-down living material. As you saw on your trip, soil is different from place to place. What are some of the properties of soil? How can you tell apart different types of soil? How does soil help plants to grow?

What are some properties of soil?

If you looked at a handful of soil, what properties could you observe? You could rub the soil between your fingers to figure out its texture. Some soil is grainy and rough. Other soil is smooth and silky. You could also observe the particles in the soil. *Particles* are small pieces of rock and other materials found in soil. You could also see the color of the soil. It might be brown, orange, tan, or another color. One other property of soil is its ability to *retain*, or keep, water.

What properties of soils allow us to sort them?

- **Particle size:** There are many different sizes of soil particles. Gravel is the largest particle in soil. Sand is smaller than gravel. The next kind of particle, silt, is smaller than sand. The smallest kind of particle is clay.

- **Texture:** Soil that has gravel in it feels rough and rocky. Sandy soil feels gritty. Soil with silt in it feels very smooth. Clay soil feels smooth and a little sticky.

- **Color:** Soils come in many colors. Some soils are dark and brown. Soils that are dark and brown usually have some materials from plants and animals that have died and broken down. Orange- or red-colored soils contain clay. Gray soils contain silt or gravel. Sandy soils have a light brown color.

If a particle of gravel were the size of a basketball …

then a particle of sand would be the size of a baseball,

a particle of silt would be the size of a golf ball,

and a particle of clay would be the size of a marble.

PROPERTIES OF SOIL

- **Ability to retain water:** Water passes easily through some soils. Soils with lots of gravel or sand do not retain water very well. Water slips past the large gravel and sand particles. Water sticks to clay particles, so soils with clay can retain a lot of water. Soil with silt also retains water well. Can you think of how plants might grow differently in these different soils?

what do you think? ·

You are studying the soil in your backyard. You notice an area of your backyard that has rocky-looking soil. Most of the particles in the soil are larger than grains of sand. The particles are gray. You observe that the soil feels rough. How would you classify the particles in this soil? Why?

What properties allow soils to support the growth of plants?

Plants grow better in some soils than others. Good soil has nutrients. It can retain water, but it also drains well. Soil with gravel or sand does not retain water well. Plants growing in this type of soil must be able to survive without much water. Gravel and sand also do not provide many nutrients to growing plants. This is why desert plants are usually smaller than plants growing in rich soil. Desert plants do not get enough water or nutrients to grow big and tall.

Soil with clay has some nutrients, but the soil keeps too much water for many plants. Water does not pass easily through clay soil—too much of it sticks around. Plants growing in soil with a lot of clay can drown. Silt has many nutrients. It is also good at retaining water—but not too much water. So, silty soils are good for farming.

Plants growing in sandy soil have to be able to survive with very little water.

The best soils for farming are usually mixtures of particle types. Adding sand or gravel to a clay or silt soil can help it drain better. Adding silt to a sandy soil contributes nutrients and helps the soil retain water. Farmers and gardeners carefully study the soil in their fields and gardens. They make sure that their plants are growing in the best soil possible.

try now

Take a few minutes to explore the properties of two different types of soil.

1. First, get two plastic cups. Ask an adult to help you poke several small holes in the bottom of each cup.

2. Collect a sample of soil from your backyard. Place the soil in one of the plastic cups.

3. Pour sand into the second cup. Make sure that both cups have equal amounts of soil or sand in them.

4. Place a paper towel under each cup. Pour the same amount of water into each cup at the same time. Watch the paper towels under the cups for signs of moisture.

5. Which paper towel got wet first? Why do you think the water passed more quickly through that soil? What does this tell you about the properties of that soil?

look out!

Broken-down rocks and decayed living things are not the only parts of soil. Soil also contains water and air. Plants need air and water to survive. Air in the soil gives plant roots room to expand and grow. Plants use water for photosynthesis. *Photosynthesis* is a process that plants use to make their own food. Without water in the soil, plants would not be able to make food.

Career Corner: Soil Scientists

Soil is almost everywhere on Earth. Scientists who study soil are called soil scientists. What do soil scientists do? Some study the soils used in farming and gardening. They figure out the best mixtures of soils for growing crops and other plants. Other soil scientists study the soil in our neighborhoods. They make sure that the ground is safe to build on and can support houses and other buildings. Other soil scientists find ways to prevent soil from blowing or washing away. Some soil scientists study areas of soil that might have precious minerals or other resources.

What does it take to be a soil scientist? You will need to study biology and physical science in school. You should also love working outdoors. You may find yourself working in tough conditions, such as in a desert or on a mountaintop.

The roots in this plant have room to grow because the soil contains air spaces. The plant also gets water and nutrients from the soil.

Accelerate Learning™

PROPERTIES OF SOIL

What Do You Know?

The table below describes the properties of different types of soil. Some parts of the table are not filled in. Use what you know about soil to fill in the missing parts. The first column asks you to describe the size of each particle. The second column asks you to describe how each type of soil feels. In the third column, describe the color of each type of soil. In the last column, describe how well each type of soil retains water.

	What is the size of the particle?	What is the texture?	What is the color?	Does it retain water well?
Gravel	Largest	Rocky		
Sand			Light brown	Not very well
Silt	Smaller than sand	Smooth		
Clay			Orange or red	Too well for many plants

Accelerate Learning™

The Soil in Your Backyard

Explore your own backyard to help your child learn more about the properties of soil. Help your child collect a soil sample from your backyard or a nearby green space. It may be interesting to take samples from several locations and compare their properties. A handful or two of soil is sufficient to collect for this activity.

Once you have collected your soil samples, spread each one out on white paper. You and your child will observe the properties of the soil in the sample. Record your observations in a notebook or on a computer.

1. First, ask your child to observe the properties that you can see, such as particle size and color.

2. Help your child classify the types of particles you see—is there any gravel, sand, clay, or silt in the sample?

3. What color is the soil? Is it dark, reddish, light brown, or gray?

4. Next, have your child rub the soil between their fingers and describe the texture of the soil.

5. Last, help your child pour a little bit of water onto the soil sample. Record what happens to the soil—does it absorb the water, or does the water pass quickly through?

Here are some questions to discuss with your child:

• What properties of the soil can you see? What is the color of the soil, and how large are the particles in the soil?

• How does the soil feel to the touch?

• Does the soil appear to be a mixture of particles, or is it all one type of particle?

• Do you think this soil would be good for growing plants? Why or why not?

reflect •

Have you ever seen a sculpture that has been outside for many years? If the sculpture is of a person, the nose and mouth might be worn down. The face might have cracks in some places. The way the sculpture looks now is probably not how it looked when the artist made it. Think of the famous Sphinx in Egypt. This sculpture was made more than 4,000 years ago. Over thousands of years, some parts of the Sphinx have worn away.

landforms: features on the surface of Earth such as mountains, dunes, valleys, oceans, and rivers

Just like structures that humans build, Earth's **landforms** change over time. Take mountains, for example. Some mountains are tall with steep slopes. They have sharp, jagged peaks. Over time, though, their slopes will become gentler. Their peaks will become more rounded and smooth, just like the face of the Sphinx. These changes happen when rocks break down and move to new places.

What forces in nature cause landforms to change? How do you think these changes happen?

What causes weathering?

One way that landforms change over time is called weathering. *Weathering* happens when forces in nature break down rocks into smaller pieces. Think of the tiny grains of sand on a beach. Those grains of sand used to be parts of larger rocks or shells. However, over time pieces of the larger rocks or shells broke off. The pieces became smaller and smaller. Now they are just tiny grains.

Weathering from ice helped create these natural arches in Utah. Over many years, parts of the rocks were worn away, leaving empty spaces.

Different things cause weathering. Wind is one way that weathering can happen. Wind carries tiny particles of soil and rock called *sediment*. As wind blows against a mountain, the sediment grinds against it. This grinding action breaks off pieces of the mountain. Liquid water can also cause weathering. Rivers carry sediment that grinds against rocks in the riverbed. Over time, large formations like canyons can form. Ice can also cause weathering. Remember that water expands when it freezes. If water seeps into cracks in rocks and then freezes, the ice pushes the cracks a little wider. After melting and refreezing many times, the ice will split the rock into pieces.

Accelerate Learning™

CHANGES TO LAND

what do you think?

The rocks at the edge of a waterfall tend to be rounded and smooth. Why do you think the rocks are this way? What caused the weathering? Where else might you see how weathering changes land?

look out!

Changes to land happen at different speeds. A volcano or an earthquake can change landforms in minutes! Wind, water, and ice are just as powerful, even though they cause changes more slowly. For example, sudden waves called *tsunamis* can uproot trees and shift whole beaches. In some cases, though, wind, water, and ice take much longer to change Earth's surface. They may even take millions of years! Look at the tall, skinny towers of rock in the picture below. They formed from an area of rock that is 30–40 million years old. The rock is still changing today. Scientists predict that in another few million years, the rock towers will appear very different.

These towering rock formations are called *hoodoos*. Short, intense rainfalls are one agent of erosion that forms these structures.

What causes erosion?

Weathering is not the only way that landforms change. When rocks break down into smaller pieces, those pieces often get moved. This movement of rock particles to a new place is called *erosion*.

Weathering and erosion work together to change Earth's surface. In fact, many things that cause weathering also cause erosion. Wind causes erosion by carrying away loose sediment from landforms like cliffs or sand dunes. In fact, sand dunes are constantly shifting positions because of wind erosion. In a similar way, running water carries away loose rock particles in a riverbed. The Colorado River, for example, has carried away enough rock

material to nearly fill the Grand Canyon! Rainwater from storms also causes erosion when it washes away soil from hillsides. Ice can also cause erosion. As a **glacier** flows downhill, it breaks off pieces of rock. The glacier then carries the rock pieces with it.

glacier: a slow-moving mass of ice

Eventually, wind, water, and ice put down the sediment they carry. This process is called *deposition*. (If you *deposit* something, you put it down.) Over time, the sediment can build up. For example, when wind stops blowing, the particles in the air fall to the ground. As more particles collect, they may build new beaches and sand dunes. Rivers may deposit sediment as they enter larger bodies of water because the water slows down. The sediment creates new land at the mouth of a river. Glaciers also deposit rock and soil as they melt and retreat.

try now •

Take some time to observe erosion and deposition in action.

Sediment piles up at the mouth of this river to form a delta.

1. To complete this activity, you will need the following materials:

   • A rectangular baking pan

   • Sand

   • Tap water

   • Two small wooden blocks

2. Place one wooden block under the edge of one side of the pan. The pan should be slightly tilted.

3. Add sand to the raised end of the pan. Make your sand like a mini beach. To do this, make sure your sand covers only about half of the pan (the higher part).

4. Pour water into the lowered end of the pan until it just reaches the edge of the beach. Do not let the water spill over the edge of the pan. If necessary, add more sand to the beach.

5. Dip the second wooden block in the water at the lowered end of the pan. Gently move it up and down to create waves.

6. Watch what happens to the sand. What signs of erosion and deposition do you see?

Looking to the Future: Threats to Forests
Human actions can also change the land. In many cases, human actions lead to erosion. For example, in recent decades, humans have cut down many large forests. People clear the land to build homes and businesses. When trees are cut down, their roots no longer hold the soil in place. As a result, the soil washes away more easily. This can be harmful for the environment. As soil erodes, nutrients that help plants grow also wash away. Fewer plants mean less food for the animals that live in the area, including humans! Also, loose soil can wash away suddenly in a landslide, which can harm other living things.

People in many areas want to make laws that protect forests. Some organizations are fighting companies around the world that are destroying forests. However, other laws are making it easier to cut down forests. For example, Brazil's government recently passed a

CHANGES TO LAND

law that allows farmers to clear some protected forests for farmland. The removal of forests continues to be a threat around the planet. Erosion can remove nutrients and important soil from areas that cannot get it back. How do you think we can prevent erosion from happening?

What Do You Know?

Landforms on Earth change in different ways. Read the list of changes in the box below. Then decide whether each change is an example of weathering, erosion, or deposition. Finally, label the agent of change in each example (wind, water, or ice).

Changes to Land	
• After a sandstorm, sand falls from the air onto a sand dune.	• Water freezes and expands inside a rock, splitting the rock into pieces.
• A creek moves sediment downstream.	• A river leaves sand and soil along the coast as it enters the ocean.
• A breeze carries small rock particles away from a mountain.	• A glacier scrapes off some sediment as it moves along a cliff.

Weathering	Erosion	Deposition

Adaptations Close to Home

To help students learn more about changes to land, take them to a nearby park. If possible, choose a park with a variety of landforms and natural features, including rivers, waterfalls, hills, and boulders. Ask students to identify as many landforms as they can.

Once students have identified the landforms, ask them to *hypothesize*, or guess, how these landforms might have changed or caused change over time. (Students have learned that wind, water, and ice cause changes to land.) Help students write down their hypotheses in a small notebook. Next, have students safely explore the landforms more closely to look for evidence of change. Students have learned about three types of changes to land: weathering (rock breaking down into smaller particles), erosion (the movement of rock particles on Earth's surface), and deposition (the settling of rock particles as they are carried by wind, water, or ice). For example, students might note that the stones along a stream bed are rounded and smooth. This is because the water carries small particles that grind down the rocks and make them smoother. Students should note whether their observations support or contradict their hypotheses about the landforms.

When you return home, research online the different landforms that students observed in the park. In particular, look for how they have changed or caused changes over time. Have students compare their observations to the information they find in their research.

Here are some questions to discuss with your child:

- How have wind, water, and/or ice affected landforms in the park?

- Did you see any signs of weathering, erosion, or deposition? If so, what kinds?

- What are some human activities that might change the landforms in the park? How would these changes affect the plants and animals that live in the area?

You use Earth's resources every day. When you eat cereal with milk for breakfast you use resources from plants and from animals. When you ride the bus to school you use fuel resources. When you take a drink of lemonade or iced tea you use water resources.

A *resource* is anything on Earth that humans use. We can use some kinds of resources over and over. Other kinds of resources can run out. What are some examples of resources on Earth? What might happen if they run out? How can we keep them from running out?

What are renewable resources?

Renewable resources can be replaced within a lifetime. Some renewable resources, such as plants and animals, provide food for humans. Other renewable resources, such as sunlight and wind, provide energy. What are some of our renewable resources?

- **Sunlight:** Sunlight is a renewable resource. The Sun will continue to shine for millions of years. We can use energy from the Sun in many important ways. Solar panels capture sunlight and turn it into electricity. Humans use this electricity to power homes and businesses.

- **Air:** Wind can be used to create electricity. Large windmills, called *turbines*, spin in fast-moving wind. The movement of the turbine's blades creates electricity.

- **Water:** Humans cannot survive without fresh water. The fresh water we use is replaced by the **water cycle**. Water is also a source of energy. Dams along rivers can use moving water to create electricity. The movement of water during tides can also provide energy.

> **water cycle:** the process by which water moves between Earth's surface and the air

Wind blowing past these turbines (top) provides us with renewable energy. Carrots (bottom) are also examples of renewable resources. Every year, new carrots grow. Humans use the carrots as a source of food.

- **Plants and Animals:** Plants provide food, energy, and useful products for humans. For example, trees provide wood. Wood can be burned to heat a home. Wood can also be turned into paper or lumber. Plants like corn, strawberries, and carrots provide food for many animals, including humans. Animals such as fish and cows also provide food.

RESOURCES

What are nonrenewable resources?

Nonrenewable resources cannot be replaced in a human lifetime. These resources take a very long time to form. When we use these resources too quickly, they can run out because there is not enough time to replace them. Three kinds of nonrenewable resources are coal, oil, and natural gas. They are called *fossil fuels* because they form from organisms that have died.

- **Coal:** Coal is a solid material that takes millions of years to form. Coal comes from plants that died millions of years ago. Thick layers of rocks and soil covered the dead plants. The pressure of the rocks and soil turned the plants into a solid called coal. Humans dig coal out of the ground. Burning coal releases its energy. We can use this energy to produce electricity.

- **Oil:** Oil is a liquid fuel that also takes millions of years to form. Oil comes from tiny animals that died in the ocean millions of years ago. Layers of mud pressed down on the dead animals. The pressure from the mud turned the dead animals into a liquid called oil. Oil can be turned into gasoline and other kinds of fuels. Oil is also used to make products such as plastics, DVDs, and tires.

This machine, called a pump jack, pulls oil up from deep under Earth's surface.

- **Natural Gas:** Natural gas forms the same way that oil does. Over millions of years, tiny dead animals are pressed down by mud and rocks. The pressure forms tiny bubbles of gas. Natural gas has no smell, but we can see it in its liquid form. It can be used to heat homes and cook food.

Look at the two photographs below. Are these examples of renewable or nonrenewable resources? Explain your answer.

How can we conserve renewable and nonrenewable resources?

Nonrenewable resources cannot be replaced in your lifetime. If we use all the coal, oil, and natural gas on Earth, there will be none left. It will take millions of years to replace these resources. How can we conserve, or save, nonrenewable resources? One solution to this problem is to use less coal, oil, and natural gas. Because they are nonrenewable, we can't replace or make more of them. Here are some ways we can use less of them: Use public transportation instead of driving a car. Turn the lights off when you leave a room. Use fabric bags instead of plastic bags at the grocery store.

Renewable resources also must be conserved. For example, trees can be used to make fuel, paper, and lumber. But what happens if you cut down all the trees in a forest? It might take many years for all of the trees to grow back. Humans should use some but not all of the renewable resources in an area. We should replace the resources we use as quickly as possible. For example, plant new trees to replace trees that are cut down.

Some renewable and nonrenewable resources can hurt the environment. Oil spills in the ocean can hurt or kill the animals living there. Burning coal releases gases and smoke into the atmosphere that can harm living things. Animal farms can create waste that drains into rivers and pollutes them. One way to stop hurting the environment is to use fewer of these resources. We can find other ways to get energy. We can also use renewable resources such as sunlight and wind power. These sources of energy create less pollution.

Accelerate Learning™

RESOURCES

• •

Some products such as gasoline or plastics are made in special factories. You might think that these resources are human-made and do not come from Earth. But all resources can be traced back to some natural material that came from Earth. Gasoline and plastic are made from oil. Oil is a nonrenewable resource that comes from Earth.

Looking to the Future: Overfishing

Fish are an example of a renewable resource. Humans eat fish for food. The human population is very big. We have many people to feed. Better technology and bigger boats allow fisherman to catch more fish than we did hundreds of years ago. But we might be catching too many fish.

Imagine that the ocean has 100 fish. What happens if we catch 90 of those fish? We will have lots of fish to eat. But only 10 fish are left to lay eggs and produce more fish.

These 10 fish cannot lay enough eggs to replace all of the fish we caught. The population of fish will start to decrease. This kind of fish might even go extinct. This is an example of overfishing. Overfishing happens when humans catch too many fish in an area. The fish population cannot survive. We have seen evidence of this in the North Atlantic Ocean. In the 1990s, humans caught too many cod. A cod is a type of fish in the Atlantic Ocean. The population of cod got so small that this fish almost went extinct. Scientists noticed the problem and stepped in. They recommended limits on the amount of cod that fisherman could catch. This allowed more adult cod to stay in the ocean and lay eggs. The population of cod began to grow again. Limiting the amount of fish that can be caught helps to keep fish populations healthy.

Accelerate Learning™

Sunlight is an example of a renewable resource. Solar panels can convert sunlight into electrical energy. To do this, solar panels need to collect as much sunlight as possible. Try this short activity to learn more about solar panel design. You will need water, two foil pie tins, black construction paper, and two thermometers.

1. Cut a piece of black construction paper to fit into one of the pie tins. Place the construction paper at the bottom of the pie tin. Leave the other pie tin as it is.

2. Pour the same amount of water into each pie tin.

3. Record the temperature of the water in each pie tin.

4. Put both pie tins in direct sunlight. Leave them in the sunlight for 20 minutes.

5. After 20 minutes, record the temperature of the water in each pie tin.

6. In which pie tin did the temperature rise the most? What does this tell you about how sunlight reacts with dark colors? If you were designing a solar panel, what color would you make it?

This house gets some of its energy from solar panels on its roof. The panels convert sunlight into electricity.

RESOURCES

What Do You Know?

Use what you know about renewable and nonrenewable resources to fill out the table below. First, decide if you agree or disagree with the statement in the left column. Then, explain why you agree or disagree in the right column.

Agree/Disagree?	Explanation
Renewable resources cannot be replaced in our lifetime. _____ Agree _____ Disagree	
Solar power, natural gas, and wood are all nonrenewable energy sources. _____ Agree _____ Disagree	
Both renewable and nonrenewable resources should be conserved. _____ Agree _____ Disagree	

Conducting a Survey

People use resources from Earth every day. Nonrenewable and renewable resources provide you with the energy, food, and products you need to live. Work with your child to create a survey that asks the people around you how they use Earth's resources. Here are some sample questions:

1. Describe how you heat your home. Do you use natural gas, oil, or another resource?

2. Where does the electricity in your home come from? Does it come from nuclear power, coal power, solar power, wind power, or another source?

3. Do you or your family members eat plant or animal products?

4. Are there any products in your home that come from nonrenewable or renewable resources? These products could include plastics, DVDs and CDs, computers, cellophane tape, air mattresses, baby oil, disposable diapers, latex gloves, petroleum jelly, firewood, paper, toothpaste, etc.

5. How do you or your family try to conserve resources?

Try to construct questions that ask about both renewable and nonrenewable resources. Conduct the survey with your neighbors, family members, or your student's classmates.

After the survey is complete, review the results with your child, and make a poster or pamphlet that describes the results.

Here are some questions to discuss with your child:

• How are people using nonrenewable and renewable resources in their daily lives?

• Which resources are used most often?

• How are people conserving resources in their daily lives?

reflect •

You are sitting in class when suddenly a loud siren sounds throughout the school. The siren means a tornado is coming! You and your classmates move into the hallway, away from windows and loose objects, and wait for the storm to pass.

How do people know a tornado is coming? Scientists use special tools to collect information about the weather on Earth. These tools help scientists predict many kinds of weather— from tornadoes to sunshine and calm breezes. What are some of the tools that scientists use? How do scientists use these tools to predict the weather?

What tools can we use to learn about the weather?

The way that the air on Earth looks and feels at a certain time and place is called weather. If someone asked you for today's weather, you might tell them how cold it is outside. You might tell them how fast the wind is blowing. These are ways of describing how the air looks and feels. Read about three special tools that scientists use to track and predict weather.

• **Wind Sock:** A wind sock helps scientists measure how fast the wind is blowing. A wind sock is made from a long tube of fabric. The tube is attached to a pole. When the wind is not blowing, the sock hangs straight down. When the wind is blowing, the sock is picked up by the wind and extends, or grows longer. How much the sock extends tells the scientists how fast the wind is blowing. The wind sock also shows the direction the wind is blowing.

• **Rain Gauge:** A rain gauge is a tool that collects rainfall. It is usually made from a tube with a funnel shape. The funnel shape helps to collect the rainwater. The tube stores the rainwater. Scientists can measure the amount of rain that has been collected. You can measure even small amounts of rainfall in rain gauges because of their funnel shape.

• **Thermometer**: A thermometer tells the temperature of the air around it. A thermometer has a long glass tube filled with liquid. As the air heats up, it also heats the liquid in the glass tube. The heated liquid expands and rises. When the liquid cools, it falls back down. There are numbers next to the glass tube that tell you what the temperature is. We measure the temperature in the United States in a unit called degrees Fahrenheit (°F). In most other countries, people measure the weather in degrees Celsius (°C). Scientists also measure temperature in degrees Celsius.

• •

WEATHER

Scientists use a tool called an *anemometer* to measure the speed of wind. You can make your own anemometer. You will need a pencil, a pushpin, a straw, and scissors. You will also need two small paper cups.

1. Ask an adult to help you poke one hole in the side of each paper cup. Stick the straw through both holes, so that one cup is on either side of the straw. The cups need to face opposite directions. The open end of one cup should face toward you. The open end of the other cup should face away from you.

2. Hold the pencil so that the eraser points at the ceiling. Place the straw across the eraser. Make sure the center of the straw is over the eraser.

3. Use the pushpin to attach the straw to the pencil's eraser. Make sure that the straw can rotate. If it cannot, you may need a longer pushpin.

4. Take your anemometer outside. Hold the anemometer in the air and see if it turns. Is the wind blowing? Does the wind speed change over time?

5. Come back the next day and hold your anemometer in the same spot. How has the wind speed changed from yesterday?

Top: This anemometer measures wind speed. As the wind blows faster, the anemometer spins more quickly. Bottom: Make your own anemometer using paper cups, a straw, and a pencil.

what do you think?

Look at the three photos show below. Which tools would you use to measure the weather conditions in each photo? Explain why you would use each tool.

look out! •

Weather and climate are not the same thing. Weather changes every day. It might rain today and be sunny tomorrow. *Climate* describes patterns of weather over a long period of a time in an area. To describe climate, a person might say that an area has very hot, dry summers. They would not describe the different kinds of weather on each day of the summer. Your weather is just what is happening on that particular day.

How does a weather map show weather conditions?

Have you ever looked at a road map? A road map uses numbers, symbols, and lines to tell you about the area you are driving through. A weather map is like a road map. It has special symbols and markings. These symbols and markings represent weather data. Scientists use weather maps to show current and future weather conditions.

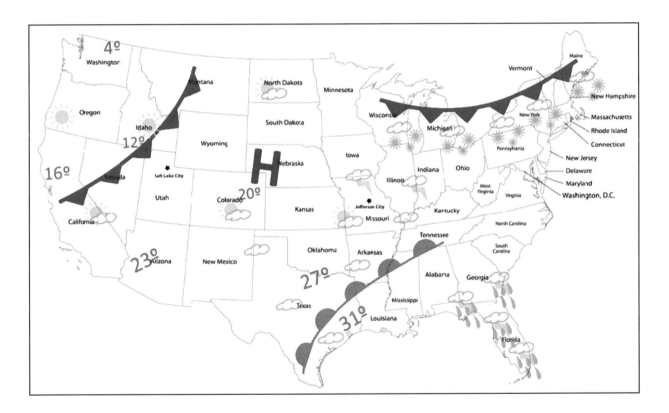

Look at the weather map shown above. Temperature is shown using numbers and the degree symbol (°). The light blue and yellow symbols represent sunny skies, cloudy skies, rain, thunderstorms, and snow. You can also see the letter "H." Some weather maps also include the letter "L." These letters represent the *air pressure* in that area.

What is air pressure? When sunlight hits Earth, some areas of air heat up more quickly than others. When warm air rises it creates an area of low pressure. "L" stands for a low pressure area on the weather map. "H" stands for a high pressure area. High pressure happens when an area of air cools and sinks back down to Earth.

• •

WEATHER

The curved lines with triangles and half-circles represent *fronts*. What is a front? A cold front, shown in blue with triangles, is a fast-moving area of cold air. Think of the wintertime. You may have felt a cold front move through your area. A warm front, shown in red with half-circles, is a fast-moving area of warm-air.

How can we use weather maps to predict weather?

Scientists use many different tools to predict weather. Computers, satellite images, and weather stations can help to predict weather. Weather maps are also important tools. Suppose a map shows that a warm front is moving toward your state. The map also shows that your state currently has cool air sitting over it.

Scientists know how cool and warm air *interact*, or influence each other. They also understand how wind speed, temperature, and other factors change the weather conditions. They can use the information on a weather map to predict the weather. When the warm front meets the cool air, you will probably see rain and cloudy skies in your area.

Scientists in the Spotlight: Casey Curry

Do you like studying and predicting the weather? Do you like speaking in front of people? Then perhaps you should be a television meteorologist. A *meteorologist* is a scientist who studies weather. Casey Curry is the meteorologist for a television station in Houston, Texas. Curry had to go to school to become a meteorologist. She took classes in science and weather. She also studied journalism to learn how to talk in front of others.

Curry does an important job for the Houston area. She predicts local weather to help people plan their days and weeks. She also helps people stay aware of severe weather like storms or heavy rain. Houston sometimes experiences dangerous thunderstorms, tornadoes, droughts, and hurricanes. Curry helps communicate with the people in her city and teach them about the weather.

What Do You Know?
Scientists use many tools to collect data about the weather. The table on the next page shows four of these tools. Fill in the second column with a description of how each tool is used.

Type of Tool	How is this tool used?
 Wind Sock	
Rain Gauge	
Thermometer	
Weather Map	

WEATHER

Predicting the Weather

Your child will pretend to be a television meteorologist who is responsible for reporting and predicting the weather for your area.

1. First, work with your child to find or create a weather map for your local region. A local or national newspaper may have a weather map that focuses on your state or region of the country. You can also consult weather prediction websites.

2. Work with your child to decipher the weather map. What do the many symbols mean? What kind of weather is currently happening in your area and what do meteorologists predict will happen next?

3. Make a poster that recreates the weather map on a large scale, just like you would see on TV. Have your child stand in front of the weather map and interpret it for you and your family (or for friends and classmates).

4. Your child should also highlight the tools that meteorologists use to collect data about weather and to predict future weather events.

Here are some questions to discuss with your child:

- What tools do scientists use to collect data about the weather?

- What do the symbols on the weather map mean?

- What is the current weather? How is it predicted to change over the next few days?

Accelerate Learning™

Think of the last time it rained in your city. When the rain stopped, you probably saw puddles on the ground. After a few hours, though, the ground was dry again. Where did all that rainwater go?

Water on Earth does not always stay in the same place. As it rains, some water flows into rivers and lakes. Some water soaks into the ground. Some water sits in puddles and then goes back into the air. In fact, the water you saw as rain today may one day end up in a faraway ocean!

How does water move from place to place? What is the source of energy that keeps water moving?

What is the water cycle?

As water moves on Earth, it changes form. Water may change to be a solid, liquid, or gas. For example, the snow on mountain peaks melts each spring. Moisture in the air may change to a liquid and fall as raindrops. These changes are part of the water cycle. The *water cycle* is a series of changes that water goes through as it moves up in the air and back down to Earth's surface. A *cycle* is a set of steps that happen over and over again. So, the steps in the water cycle repeat without stopping.

This photo of the comet Lovejoy was taken from the International Space Station.

Discover Science: Where did Earth's water come from?
Even though water is always moving, it rarely enters or leaves our planet. In fact, the water on Earth today is the same water that the dinosaurs drank! But where did this water first come from?

Many scientists think that some of Earth's water came from *comets*. Comets are objects made of dust and ice that move through space. A certain substance found in comets is also found in Earth's oceans. This is why scientists think that comets may have brought some water to Earth.

Other scientists think that meteorites and asteroids were the source of water on our planet. Meteorites and asteroids are other types of space objects that sometimes collide with Earth. Many scientists also think that some of Earth's water came from the molten rock inside Earth. This hot rock then released water as a gas into Earth's atmosphere. Most scientists agree that water on Earth first existed as a gas. Then, when Earth went through a cooling phase, the gas changed to a liquid. The liquid water fell as rain. Then the

THE SUN AND WATER CYCLE

rain gathered in the lowest parts of Earth's surface, forming oceans. Over time, both liquid water and ice continued to flow over Earth's surface. This water formed glaciers in places that were cold enough. The water also formed rivers that cut into the land and shaped it. Moving water continues to change Earth's landscape today.

look out! •

The amount of water on Earth stays pretty much the same. So why do people worry about protecting our water supply? This is because more than 97% of water on Earth is salt water. Humans need fresh water to survive. Another problem is that most fresh water is frozen as **glaciers** and **ice caps**. Therefore, humans have a small supply of fresh water. Polluting that water makes our supply even smaller.

glacier: a slow-moving mass of ice

ice cap: a mass of ice that permanently covers a large area

How does water move through the water cycle around Earth?

Water is found in many places on Earth. Some of the easiest places to see water are oceans, rivers, and lakes. Many rivers and lakes contain fresh water. They help to supply us with water to drink. However, rivers and lakes contain a very small portion of Earth's water. Most of Earth's water is found in oceans, seas, and bays. After oceans, glaciers and ice caps make up the next largest water source. Glaciers are found in places that are cold enough to have ice all year long, such as high up in the mountains. Ice caps are found near Earth's poles.

The Aletsch Glacier, shown above, is the largest glacier in Europe. It stretches more than 45 miles!

Fog is a collection of water droplets very close to Earth's surface. Fog often makes it hard to see!

Not all water is easy to see, though. Some of Earth's water is found in the air as a gas. Have you ever stepped outside in the summer and felt muggy or sticky? That's because there is a lot of water in the air, but it's in the form of a gas. This gas is called *water vapor*. The amount of water vapor in the air is called *humidity*. That's the sticky feeling you might have experienced outside. Water vapor can come from the liquid water in oceans, lakes, and rivers. This change in water from a liquid to a gas is called *evaporation*. The same thing happens to puddles after a rainstorm. Evaporation is one step in the water cycle.

Accelerate Learning™

Another step in the water cycle is called condensation. *Condensation* happens when water vapor cools and changes into liquid water. Water vapor condenses on dust particles in the air. The small droplets of water form clouds and fog.

Sometimes the water droplets in clouds get bigger. They become too heavy, and they fall to the ground as rain. Depending on weather conditions, the water droplets may also fall as snow, sleet, or hail. Rain, snow, sleet, and hail are all forms of *precipitation*. Precipitation is an important part of the water cycle. It lets water from the air fill the oceans and lakes on Earth's surface. Rain helps refill lakes and rivers, too. These rivers flow to the oceans.

Not all precipitation goes straight to the ocean, though. Some precipitation seeps into the ground. This water is called *ground water*. Ground water flows through the spaces in rocks underground. It eventually flows into rivers, lakes, and oceans. Once it reaches these bodies of water, it continues the water cycle through evaporation.

what do you think?

Take a look at this photograph. What step in the water cycle does this picture show? Where was the water before this step? What will happen to the water after this step?

What is the major source of energy that moves water through the water cycle?
Water cannot move through the water cycle on its own. It needs **energy** to do so. The main source of energy for the water cycle is the Sun. The Sun's heat powers the water cycle in different ways. But how does this work?

> **energy:** what is needed to do work or cause change

First, heat causes water to change form. As the Sun warms oceans and lakes, the liquid water becomes water vapor. Second, the Sun heats the air, which causes the air to move. This moving air is called *wind*. Wind moves water vapor to another place. If the water vapor hits cooler air, it will condense and form clouds. In addition, the Sun's heat affects air temperature. In turn, air temperature affects what type of precipitation falls. If the air is warm, rain will fall. If the air is cold enough, sleet or snow will fall.

Just as the wind moves this sailboat, it carries water vapor from place to place. In this way, wind is part of the water cycle.

try now

THE SUN AND WATER CYCLE

Does salt water evaporate? Find out by doing this activity.

1. You will need the following materials:
   - a large, clear bowl
   - a small pitcher
   - a clear glass
   - plastic wrap
   - a large rubber band
   - a small rock
   - tap water
   - salt
   - a spoon

2. Place the glass in the large bowl. The rim of the glass should be shorter than the rim of the bowl.

3. Add some water to the small pitcher. Use the spoon to stir in some salt.

4. Gently pour the salt water into the bowl. The glass should stay empty.

5. Cover the bowl with plastic wrap. Fix it in place with the rubber band.

6. Place the rock on top of the plastic wrap. It should be just over the top of the glass. The plastic wrap should now slope down toward the glass.

7. Place the bowl on a sunny windowsill. Observe the bowl after about 30 minutes. Do you see anything on the plastic wrap? If so, why?

8. After a few hours, take the plastic wrap off of the bowl. Taste the water inside the glass.

9. Is the water salty? Why or why not? How did the water get inside the glass?

What do you know?

The steps in the water cycle happen over and over again. Look at the steps of the water cycle in the box. Then add the steps to the diagram in the correct order.

Steps in the Water Cycle	
• Wind moves water vapor to an area of cooler air.	• Water evaporates and becomes water vapor.
• Water flows underground to an ocean.	• Water flows in a river to an ocean.
• Water droplets get heavy and fall as precipitation.	• Water droplets hang in the air as a cloud.
	• Water vapor condenses on dust particles

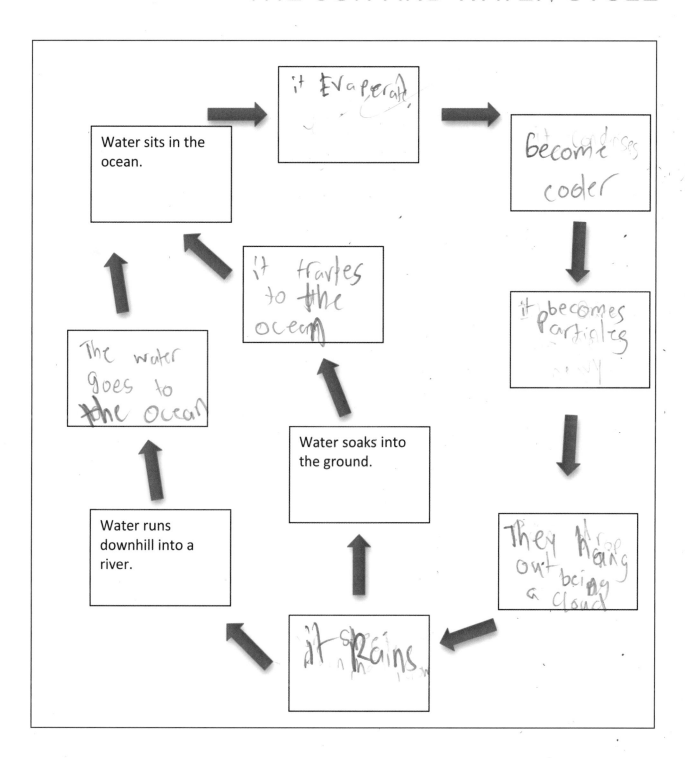

it Evaperat

Become coder

Water sits in the ocean.

it becomes Particles ...

it travles to the ocean

The water goes to the Ocean

Water soaks into the ground.

They drop out being a cloud

Water runs downhill into a river.

it Rains

THE SUN AND WATER CYCLE

A Water Cycle Photo Journal

To help students reinforce what they have learned about the water cycle, have them make a photo journal recording ways that they observe the water cycle in their daily lives. First, review with your child the various ways that water moves through the water cycle. Your child has learned about *evaporation* (liquid water becomes water vapor), *condensation* (water vapor becomes liquid water), and *precipitation* (liquid or solid water that falls from the sky). Next, brainstorm places where you might find evidence of each of these processes, and instruct students to take pictures of these places and other places that they encounter over the course of a week. For example, they might take pictures of the following things:

- *Condensation*: clouds; droplets on the side of a cold glass; dew on the grass

- *Evaporation*: puddles drying in sunlight; dishes or clothes drying in the air

- *Precipitation*: rain or snow

At the end of the week, have your child compile the pictures in a printed or digital photo journal. Help your child write captions for each picture describing how water is moving through the water cycle in that picture. Encourage your child to use the words *condense/condensation*, *evaporate/evaporation*, and *precipitation* in the captions.

Here are some questions to discuss with your child:

- Where are some places you can find water on Earth?

- How does water enter the air? How does it return to Earth's surface?

- How is the Sun involved in the water cycle?

reflect

Have you ever made shadow puppets? If you put your hand between a flashlight and a wall, you will make a shadow. You might have made a rabbit shape or some other animal shape with your hands. Your hand blocks the light from the flashlight.

The Sun shines on Earth like a giant flashlight. Light from the Sun causes shadows that we can see here on Earth. The angle of the Sun's light also causes the change in seasons: from winter to spring to summer to fall. How else does Earth interact with the Sun?

How do shadows change during the seasons?
Shadows are formed when an object blocks light. For example, when sunlight hits the metal piece on this sundial, it forms a shadow. The shadow can be used to tell the time of day. That is because shadows change shape during the day. When the Sun first rises, it sits very low on the horizon. Sunlight hits objects at an angle that creates long shadows. In the middle of the day, the Sun sits directly above. Sunlight hits objects at an angle that creates very small shadows. As the Sun sets near the horizon, it creates long shadows again. Those shadows point in different directions, though, making a sundial useful for telling time.

A sundial uses shadows to tell time. Sunlight hits a metal piece sticking out of the flat sundial. The shadow from the metal piece points to a number. This sundial is telling you it is 3:00 in the afternoon.

The shape of shadows also depends on which season it is. Earth's axis is tilted slightly off-center. During our summer, the northern half of Earth is tilted, or leaning, toward the Sun. So, the Sun's light hits the northern half of Earth at a more direct angle. Because the Sun is more directly overhead, shadows are smaller in the summer than in the winter. In the winter, the northern part of Earth is tilted away from the Sun. That means the sunlight is not coming in as directly. So, shadows during the winter are longer. Imagine that you stood in the same spot at 3:00 p.m. in the winter and in the summer. Your shadow would look longer in the winter.

what do you think?

What time of day do you think it is in the first picture? What time of day do you think it is in the second picture? Explain your answers.

PATTERNS ON EARTH

• •

Take a few minutes to collect and analyze data in order to predict seasonal changes in your area.

A change in temperature is one way to show that a new season is coming. As a scientist, your job is to collect data to predict patterns of change in things over time, like seasons. Go online and locate the high and low temperatures in your area for each month for the last three years. When did each season occur? How can you tell? Analyze these data and see if you can find a pattern. Use this information to predict the time of the next season change in your area.

look out! •

You may think that seasons happen because Earth is farther away from the Sun in winter or closer to the Sun in summer. This is not correct. Earth stays at almost the same distance from the Sun all year. Seasons happen because Earth is tilted on its axis. During summer, the northern part of Earth is tilted toward the Sun. The Sun's light hits the northern part of Earth more directly. The heat from the sunlight causes the warm weather of summer. During winter, the northern part of Earth is tilted, or leaning away from the Sun. The Sun's light does not shine as directly, causing cooler weather.

How do the positions of Earth and the Moon affect tides on Earth?

If you stand on a beach for several hours, you will see the tide coming in and out. The *tide* is the rise and fall of ocean water over a period of time. Tides rise and fall every day—sometimes even twice a day. But what causes tides?

Look up into the night sky and you might see the Moon. The Moon *orbits* Earth. This means that the Moon moves around Earth in a path shaped like a circle. The Moon and Earth pull on each

> **gravity:** the force that attracts one thing with mass to another thing with mass

other due to **gravity**. When the Moon pulls on Earth, the solid parts of Earth stay in place. They cannot move very much. But the water in the oceans can move more easily. The Moon's gravity pulls the ocean water toward it. This causes a bulge in the ocean in the direction of the Moon. This bulge is what causes a high tide. Ocean water comes up higher on a shoreline as it is pulled toward the Moon. As the ocean is pulled toward the Moon, it causes a low tide in another part of Earth.

How does the Moon's appearance in the sky change?

We are able to see the Moon because it reflects light from the Sun. Have you noticed how the Moon's shape changes during the month? The Moon seems to get bigger, and then it seems to get smaller. Sometimes, it seems to disappear completely.

orbit: the circular path of one object around another object

These changes happen in the same pattern each month. In fact, you can predict them! The Sun always shines on half of the Moon. But on Earth, we cannot always see the sunlit half. This is because the Moon moves around Earth in an **orbit**. At the beginning of each month, we cannot see the Moon at all. The sunlit half of the Moon faces away from Earth. Each night we see more of the Moon. After about two weeks, we can see the entire sunlit half of the Moon. Then, the Moon seems to get smaller again. Each night we see less and less. At the end of the month, we cannot see the Moon at all again. The pattern then repeats itself.

As the Moon orbits Earth, we see different parts of it. At the beginning and end of each month, we see very little of the Moon. Midway through each month, we see a large part of the Moon.

Accelerate Learning™

PATTERNS ON EARTH

Discover Science: Ancient Cultures
Humans have noticed patterns on Earth for a very long time. For example, ancient Romans used sundials to tell time. The Romans noticed that the length and shape of shadows changed over the course of a day. They built sundials to allow them to keep track of the hours in a day.

Ancient Chinese people used the Moon's changing appearance to make a calendar. Each month was 29 days—the amount of time it takes the Moon to orbit Earth. The beginning of a month was marked by a new moon. This calendar is still used to keep track of Chinese holidays.

What Do You Know?
The Moon, Earth, and Sun interact in many different ways. That means they affect each other, or cause changes to each other. These interactions cause patterns on Earth that we can predict. The graphic organizer below describes some of these patterns. It is missing some information. Use the words in the box below to fill in the missing parts of the graphic organizer:

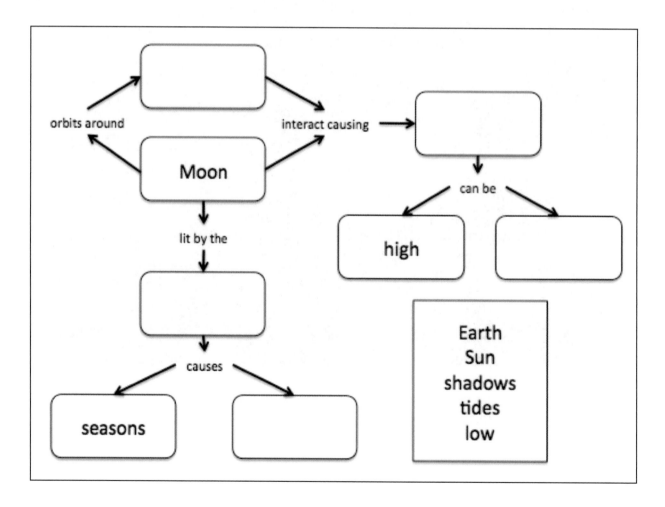

Modeling the Lunar Cycle

Actively modeling the phases of the Moon can help students understand how and why the Moon's appearance changes throughout the month. (Students at this level have not yet learned the term *phases*, so do not use it when explaining this activity. Simply talk about the Moon when it is larger and the Moon when it is smaller.) This activity will allow students to act as "Earth" and model the phases of the Moon. For this activity, you will need the following materials:

- A pencil
- A foam ball (or any lightly colored, spherical object, such as a baseball)
- A lamp with a removable lampshade

Remove the shade from the lamp so only the bare bulb is showing. Turn the lamp on, but be careful that neither you nor your child stares directly at the bulb. Place the pointed end of the pencil into the foam ball and have your child grasp the pencil as a handle. Explain to your child that the foam ball represents the Moon and the light bulb represents the Sun; your child represents Earth.

First, have your child face the light bulb from about 1 m away, and make sure the foam ball is between your child's body and the light. The foam ball should appear dark from your child's perspective. This position demonstrates the new moon phase—the "Sun" is illuminating the half of the "Moon" that faces away from Earth. Next, have your child rotate slowly about 90 degrees to the right. The foam ball should gradually become illuminated, and by the 90 degree

mark, half of the "Moon" should appear to be lit by the "Sun." Then, have your child rotate another 90 degrees so that the "Sun" is directly behind them. Make sure your child holds the foam ball slightly overhead so that your child's body does not obstruct the light. This position represents the full moon phase. Make another 90 degree turn and observe how the illumination of the foam ball changes. Finally, have your child return to the new moon phase.

Here are some questions to discuss with your child:

- In the model, what did the Moon look like to Earth when it was between the Sun and Earth? When in the month does this happen?
- How did the light on the Moon change as Earth rotated?
- Was half of the Moon always illuminated by the Sun?
- Could the illuminated half of the Moon always be seen from Earth? Why or why not?

PRODUCERS, CONSUMERS, AND FOOD WEBS

• •

Think about the last meal you ate. Where did the food come from? Maybe it came from the grocery store or a restaurant. Maybe it even came from your backyard. Now think of a lion living on the plains in Africa. Where do you think his last meal came from? Definitely not the grocery store! Lions have to hunt for their food.

Most humans do not hunt for their food. But humans and lions have something in common. Both eat other living things. In this way, humans and lions have a similar relationship to their **ecosystem**. In fact, scientists group living things based on how they get food. By studying how **organisms** get food, scientists understand how **energy** moves through an ecosystem. This flow of energy from one organism to the next forms a *food chain*. What are some types of food in a food chain? What happens if some of these food sources change or disappear?

> **ecosystem:** a community of living and nonliving things in their natural environment

> **organism:** a living thing

> **energy:** what is needed to do work or cause change

What are producers? What do they need to make their food?

Some living things make their own food. These organisms are called *producers*. Plants are producers. They use sunlight, water, and a gas called carbon dioxide to make sugars. The plants use these sugars for energy to grow and survive.

Producers are always the first organism in a food chain. They provide energy for other living things in the food chain. Even though not all animals eat producers, all animals rely on producers to change sunlight into usable energy.

Most bears are omnivores. They eat plants like grasses and berries. They also eat meat such as fish.

What are consumers? Where do they get their food?

Many living things cannot make their own food. These organisms are called consumers. If they don't make their own food, where do you think it comes from? *Consumers* get energy by eating other organisms. There are several different types of consumers. Some consumers are herbivores. *Herbivores* eat only plants or other plant-like producers called algae. Other consumers, called *carnivores*, eat only other animals. Some consumers eat both plants and other animals. These consumers are called *omnivores*.

• •

PRODUCERS, CONSUMERS, AND FOOD WEBS

what do you think?

People are consumers, not producers, because they eat other organisms. Think of the things people eat. What type of consumers are we? Are people carnivores, herbivores, or omnivores? Do you think some people might be in different categories? Why?

Where does the energy come from that starts a food chain?

As one organism eats another, energy moves through a food chain. But where does the energy first come from? The energy that starts a food chain comes from the Sun. Producers use sunlight to make energy for other organisms that they can use. Can we make our own food from sitting in the Sun? Not at all! When a consumer like yourself eats plants, the energy that first came from the Sun passes on to the consumer. When another consumer eats the plant-eater, the energy passes on again.

What is a food web?

In a food chain, the energy seems to flow in a straight line from one organism to the next. In reality though, energy in an ecosystem flows in many directions. This is because most consumers rely on more than one type of food. For this reason, a food web is a better way to show these relationships. A *food web* is a connection of food chains with many food energy paths in an ecosystem. Just as in a food chain, the energy that starts a food web comes from the Sun.

In the food web shown at the right, the Sun's energy flows to algae. The algae make their own food using sunlight, water, and carbon dioxide.

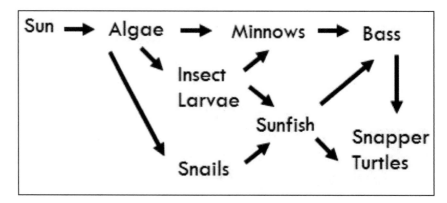

Next, the energy flows to organisms that eat algae, such as minnows, insect **larvae**, and snails. Then the energy flows to larger consumers, such as bass, sunfish, and snapper turtles.

larvae: the young, newly hatched form of certain insects

PRODUCERS, CONSUMERS, AND FOOD WEBS

look out! •

The arrows in a food web diagram show the flow of energy. The first arrow always starts at the Sun, which is the source of energy. The arrows point to the next organism that uses that energy. That means arrows point from the source of energy to whatever consumes that energy. For example, the arrow that points from snails to sunfish shows that snails provide energy to sunfish. In other words, sunfish eat snails.

try now •

Do different food chains have similar structures? Find out with this activity.

1. To complete this activity, you will need the following materials:
   - construction paper: yellow, green, blue, purple, and red
   - scissors
   - tape
   - a marker
   - a ruler

2. Cut the construction paper into strips about two inches wide.

3. Look at the food web above. Choose one food chain from this food web.

4. Write each part of the food chain on a different strip of paper. Use different colored strips according to the role of each thing in the food chain. If you don't have different colored paper, just use different colored markers. Use this color code: original energy source = yellow, producer = green, herbivore = blue, omnivore = purple, carnivore = red.

5. Make a paper chain that connects each strip in order. Do this by taping together the ends of the first strip. It should make a loop. Next, put the second strip through the loop. Tape the ends together to make a second loop. Continue with the rest of the strips.

6. Repeat Steps 3–5 with two more food chains from the food web.

7. Look at your three paper food chains. Do you notice any patterns in the colors? What color is at the beginning of the chains? What color is at the end of the chains? How do the colors show the flow of energy?

How do changes in an ecosystem affect a food web in an ecosystem?

Changes to an ecosystem can affect the flow of energy in food webs. For example, a forest fire may destroy tall trees and logs in an ecosystem. As a result, small animals that live in the trees either move or die. So the number of small animals, such as bats and squirrels, in that ecosystem gets smaller.

There are more changes that can happen. If there are fewer small animals, the food supply decreases for the carnivores that eat them. As a result, fewer of these carnivores can survive in the ecosystem. A single change affects all the living things in a food web.

Looking to the Future: The Golden-Cheeked Warbler in Danger

In many cases, human actions change ecosystems. For example, humans cut down juniper and oak trees in central Texas. These trees are home to a type of bird called the golden-cheeked warbler. Now the birds are in danger because they are losing their living spaces. Today, there only about 2,100 golden-cheeked warblers. If the bird becomes **extinct**, the ecosystem will change even more.

> **extinct:** having no living members

Golden-cheeked warblers eat insects like caterpillars and beetles. This helps to control the insect population. If the warbler populations decrease, the number of insects will grow. Think about how having more insects would change the plants in the forest! Caterpillars and beetles eat the leaves of many different plants. If too many insects live in an area, they will eat way more of the plants.

Fortunately, many people are working to protect the golden-cheeked warbler. The warblers now have a protected national wildlife area in Texas. This protection helps keep some balance in the warbler's food web.

PRODUCERS, CONSUMERS, AND FOOD WEBS

What Do You Know?

Read about the parts of a grassland food web in the chart below. Use the information from the chart to complete the food web diagram. Fill in each box with the correct organism. Then label each organism in the food web diagram as a producer or a consumer.

Grassland Food Web	
Organism	**How it gets energy**
snake	eats grasshoppers
hawk	eats snakes and sparrows
sparrow	eats grasshoppers and spiders
grasshopper	eats grass
grass	makes its own food
spider	eats grasshoppers

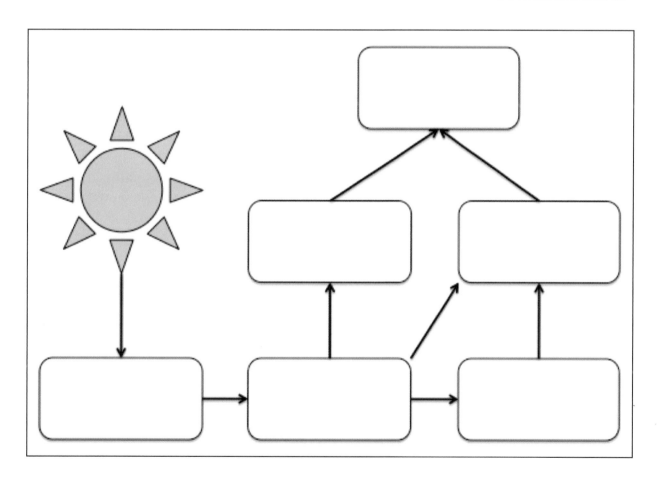

PRODUCERS, CONSUMERS, AND FOOD WEBS

What's in Our Food Web?

To help students learn more about food webs, prepare a meal with them. Try to use a recipe that includes mainly unprocessed ingredients, as it will be easier to find the origin of natural products. As you prepare the meal, discuss with students the origin of each ingredient. Have them identify whether the source of each ingredient is a producer or a consumer. Examples of common producer ingredients include fruits, nuts, and vegetables. Examples of common consumer ingredients include dairy products and meats. If you are unsure about the origin of an ingredient, write it down and research it online with students later.

After the meal, make a food web with students. The food web should include the ingredients you worked with to prepare the meal. Look online to find other animals that eat the ingredients, and include the animals in the food web. Help students draw arrows between the parts of the food web to show the flow of energy. (An arrow should begin at the food being eaten and point to the consumer of the food.) Make sure students include the Sun in the food web. The Sun provides energy for the plants in the food web, so draw arrows from the Sun to each plant. Students can draw each component of the food web, or they can cut out pictures and paste them on the poster board. Have students label each component as a producer or consumer.

Here are some questions to discuss with students:

- What are the producers in the food web you created? What are the consumers?

- Where does energy start in the food web?

- What are some different paths in this food web that connect the Sun's energy to us?

A penguin swims through icy cold waters. It has special feathers that layer like shingles on a roof. These tightly packed feathers keep out cold water and keep its body heat in. The penguin also has special types of eyes. The lenses in its eye help it see above and below the water. Its powerful wings help it swim through the water. The penguin's feet help it steer as it swims.

> **predator:** an animal that hunts and eats other animals

Being able to stay warm, see well, and swim quickly helps the penguin find food and avoid predators. What are some other characteristics that help animals survive in their environment?

What is meant by adaptation?

An *adaptation* is any characteristic that helps a plant or animal survive in its environment. A penguin's feathers are an adaptation. The feathers keep the penguin warm. Where do adaptations come from? They develop over long periods of time. It takes many generations for adaptations to develop. Adaptations usually have something to do with where an organism lives. For example, animals that live in cold places have adaptations to keep them warm. Plants that live in dry areas have adaptations to help them conserve water.

How do external adaptations help organisms survive in their environment?

A penguin's strong wings are an external adaptation. *External* means on the outside, or something you can see. Here are some examples of external adaptations:

- **Bird beaks:** Birds use their beaks to collect and eat food. A bird's beak is an adaptation to the type of food it eats. Beaks come in all shapes and sizes. For example, a hawk has a sharp, curved beak. This sharp beak helps it tear its food into small pieces. A hummingbird has a long, thin beak. This helps the hummingbird reach into flowers and suck up nectar. A pelican has a long beak with a pouch. This beak helps it scoop fish out of the water.

- **Plant leaves:** Just like animals, plants must be adapted to their environment in order to survive. Plant leaves are an important part of the plant. Plants need to absorb sunlight through leaves to make their own food. Also, water can escape from the plant through the leaves. So, plants that live in dry climates usually have small leaves. The leaves may also be coated in thick wax. This prevents the plant from drying out. Plants in sunny, moist climates have big, wide leaves. Big leaves absorb lots of sunlight. In windy, cold climates, plants are usually short with small leaves. Short plants are more protected from wind. Some plants protect themselves with poison. Their leaves contain oils that annoy or even kill an organism that tries to eat the leaves.

ADAPTATIONS

- Camouflage: *Camouflage* is an adaptation that helps animals hide. Animals with camouflage look just like their environment. Camouflage allows an animal to hide

from predators or to sneak up on **prey**. The mimic octopus is able to change the color of its skin. It can look like any object it is sitting near. This helps the octopus avoid being eaten. Lion fur is the same color as the dry grass in which a lion hunts. Being camouflaged allows lions to approach prey without being seen.

> **prey:** an animal that is killed and eaten by another animal

try now

Plants that live in dry, hot climates have thick, waxy leaves. The wax prevents water from leaving the plant. This activity demonstrates how wax protects a plant leaf. You will need two small pieces of white construction or notebook paper, a bowl of water, and a crayon.

1. Draw on both sides of one piece of paper with the crayon. Try to cover as much of the surface as you can, leaving none of the paper showing. Leave the other piece of paper exactly as it is.

2. Put both pieces of paper into the bowl of water. Observe what happens to the papers as they touch the water. Did water soak into both of the papers?

3. Crayons are made from wax. How did this activity model the way in which wax protects plant leaves from losing water?

what do you think?

Look at the picture on the right. It shows a bird that lives in a cold, snowy, place. What are some external adaptations that allow this bird to survive? Do you think this bird could survive in a hot, dry, sandy desert? Explain.

look out !

Organisms cannot choose their adaptations. For example, an animal living in a cold environment cannot just choose to grow thick fur. Adaptations develop over time. They are passed down from generation to generation. Animals with adaptations that help them survive pass these adaptations onto their young.

How do internal adaptations help organisms survive in their environment?

Plants, animals, and other living things have adaptations that you cannot see. These adaptations are called *internal* adaptations. For example, some animals hibernate.

A hibernating animal goes to sleep or is dormant during cold weather. They do not have to hunt for food. They just rest until springtime. This adaptation allows animals such as bears to survive the winter. Some animals are warm blooded. This adaptation allows them to keep their body temperature the same, no matter how hot or cold it is outside. Humans are also warm blooded, as are all mammals.

Plants have internal adaptations, too. Some plants have special chemicals in their cells that help them grow toward sunlight. Plants also have an adaptation that allows them to make their own food inside their cells.

Everyday Life: Wisdom Teeth

Some adaptations are useful and are passed down from generation to generation. Other adaptations become less useful as the environment changes. An example of an adaptation that may no longer be useful is wisdom teeth. Wisdom teeth are the teeth all the way at the back of your mouth. They are a type of molar. A molar is a thick, flat tooth used to grind food. If you tried to see your wisdom teeth, you could not. At your age, your wisdom teeth are hidden in your gums. They do not usually appear until you are at least 15 years old. Wisdom teeth were useful to ancient humans. Long ago, humans ate tough food that wore down their regular molars. Wisdom teeth could replace molars that had been worn down. But now, humans cook food. Our teeth do not wear

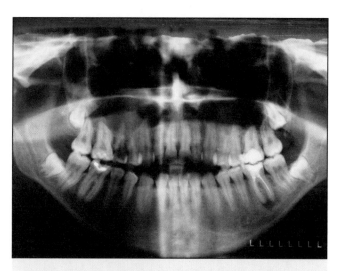

This person still has wisdom teeth. They are the white teeth on the left and right sides of this x-ray.

down as quickly. Some dentists suggest taking out wisdom teeth with surgery. They say that wisdom teeth are an adaptation that we no longer need.

ADAPTATIONS

What Do You Know?

The table on the next page lists plant and animal adaptations. Each list of adaptations has one item that does not belong. Circle the item that does not belong. Use the space in the right column to explain why the item doesn't belong.

Which item does not belong?	Why doesn't this item belong?
Hard turtle shell Sharp, curved beak Hibernation	
Camouflage Small leaves covered in thick wax Poisonous leaves	
An octopus that can change color Warm-blooded An insect that looks exactly like a twig	

• •

Hunting for Hidden Animals

To help students learn more about adaptations, have them practice hunting "prey" that are camouflaged. Students will pretend to be birds hunting prey in your backyard or local green space.

1. You will need string, pipe cleaners, or yarn in four different colors. Three of the colors should be bright, loud hues that are easy to see on the grass. The fourth color should be similar to the color of your lawn or green space. You will also need a stopwatch or timer and a bag for each student.

2. Cut the string, pipe cleaners, or yarn into four-inch pieces. Scatter the pieces in a large area of your yard such as a 10 meter by 10 meter area. This will be the hunting zone. Try to make sure the four different colors are equally distributed in the hunting zone. Make sure students are not watching you as you spread out the items.

3. Tell students they will have 30 seconds to hunt for as many of the "prey" items as they can and place them in the bag. While students hunt, they must move constantly through the hunting area, except for when they stop to pick up an item. After 30 seconds, count how many of the brightly colored prey items students were able to pick up.

4. Next, give students 30 seconds to hunt for the prey items that are the same color as the yard or the green space. As before, students must move constantly through the hunting area, except for when they stop to pick up an item. After 30 seconds, count how many of these prey items students were able to pick up.

Here are some questions to discuss with students:

- What kind of adaptation allows animals to blend into the environment around them?

- Which color represented camouflaged animals?

- Which type of "prey" were you able to catch the most of?

- How does camouflage help animals avoid being eaten?

You can use other kinds of colored objects, such as these playground balls.

• •

Accelerate Learning™

• •

Look at the mother polar bear and her cub. What are some things they have in common? They both have thick fur that looks white. They both have black noses. Both bears have large paws with sharp claws.

The two bears also have things in common that you cannot see in the picture. The mother and her cub hunt seals for food. They are both good swimmers. They also have an excellent sense of smell.

offspring: the child or offshoot from a parent

trait: an internal or external characteristic or feature

Parents and **offspring** of other organisms are also alike in many ways. They share certain features, or **traits**. Many of these traits help organisms survive in their environment. For example, a polar bear's fur helps it blend in with the snow and keep it warm in its cold habitat. Her sense of smell helps the mother bear find food when she is hunting.

Why do parents and offspring have so many traits in common? How are these traits passed from one generation to the next?

What features do organisms inherit from their parents?
Many living things inherit, or get, certain traits from their parents. *Inherited* traits are passed from parent to offspring during **reproduction**. Many external features of an organism are inherited. This is why different groups of organisms look so different. Think about types of birds. A flamingo inherits long legs and a long, curved neck from its parents. An eagle inherits sharp claws and a sharp, curved beak from its parents. Plants also pass on inherited traits such as leaf shape and size. For example, a maple leaf is wide. A fern leaf is long and narrow. These leaf shapes are inherited from the parent tree.

reproduction: the process by which parents make offspring

• •

Accelerate Learning™

TRAITS

Some inherited traits are not how it looks, but instead what an organism can do. For example, some organisms, such as plants, inherit the ability to make their own food. Cats such as lions and tigers inherit the desire to hunt for food. House cats may hunt birds or mice, even though their owners give them pet food! Scientists think that even facial expressions are inherited. People who are born blind still naturally smile and frown, even without seeing other people do it.

What features are learned behaviors?
Not all features are passed from parent to offspring. Think of animals that can do tricks. Some dogs will sit, stay, or roll over if humans give them commands. Some dolphins can jump through rings. These behaviors did not come from the organisms' parents. These behaviors are learned. Learned behaviors are changes made by an organism in response to its environment.

Parents or other adults can help teach their offspring learned behavior. For example, human parents often teach children certain manners, like sitting up straight or saying please. Children are not born with these manners. They have to learn them. The same is true about reading. Reading is not an inherited trait. Adults teach other humans to read.

what do you think? • • • • • • • • • • • • • • • • •

Look at the picture of the seal. What is one feature that the seal inherited from its parents? What is one feature that it learned?

look out! •

Many parts of an organism's physical appearance are inherited. However, some physical features are not inherited. For example, if an organism cuts or burns itself, it may develop a scar. This scar did not come from its parents. The same is true of a broken bone or dying your hair a different color. Those changes came from an interaction with the environment. This physical feature will not pass on to the next generation. Think of your own physical features. Do you have any that came from interactions with the environment?

Accelerate Learning™

try now •

Let's learn about inherited traits and learned behaviors in your class.

1. Which of these traits or behaviors do you have? Write your answers on a piece of paper.

   - have dimples/don't have dimples

   - can play an instrument/can't play an instrument

   - have freckles/don't have freckles

   - can roll tongue/can't roll tongue

   - have hanging earlobes/have attached earlobes

   - have a scar/don't have a scar

   - can ride a bicycle/can't ride a bicycle

2. Compare your answers with a partner. Are their differences in your answers?

3. With your partner, discuss which features are inherited and which are learned. Check your answers with your teacher or ask an adult to help you find the answer online.

4. If possible, count how many people in your class have each feature. Which features are the most common?

Career Corner: Animal Breeders

Why do some sheep produce more wool than others? Why do some dogs have floppy ears and some have pointed ears? In many cases, humans have changed the traits these animals have over time. Humans that work with animals' inherited traits are called animal breeders. Animal breeders change inherited traits by choosing which animals should reproduce. The breeders choose animals that have valuable traits. The goal is for these parents to pass on their valuable traits to their offspring. Sometimes breeders choose two parents with very different features in order to produce offspring with a unique mix of traits.

Animal breeders work with many different types of animals. For example, they breed horses to produce offspring that are very fast and can run in horse races. Animal breeders also breed farm animals. They try to create offspring that produce more of the goods that humans use, such as milk and wool. Breeders also work with threatened species in zoos. They try to make sure the animals produce offspring. In this way, they try to help the species continue.

• •

TRAITS

What Do You Know?
Look at the pictures of the organisms below. Find the features from the box that match the organism in each picture. Decide whether each feature is inherited or learned. Write the feature in the correct column next to the matching organism.

Features	
• plays football	• stays on command
• curly hair	• jumps through a hoop
• balances on a ball	• fins on the back and tail
• reddish-brown hair	• wrinkled, gray skin

Organism	Inherited	Learned

Family Traits Interview

To help students learn more about inherited traits and learned behaviors, have them interview a parent and child you know who are biologically related. Before the interview, brainstorm a list of questions to ask about inherited traits and learned behaviors. Recall that inherited traits are features passed genetically from parent to child and learned behaviors are actions that a child learns to do from experience or instruction. For example, students may ask about inherited traits like eye color, hair color, hair texture, or dimples. They may ask about learned behaviors such as playing sports or instruments. Students should ask the parent and child the same questions in order to compare their traits and behaviors. Make sure students do not ask about any issues that are too personal or sensitive. You may wish to share the questions beforehand with the relative you are interviewing.

Go with students to conduct the interview. Have students record their responses in a notebook. After the interview, help students complete a Venn diagram showing which features the parent and child share and which features they do not.

Here are some questions to discuss with students:

- In what ways are the parent and child alike? Which of these features are inherited and which are learned?
- Why might the parent and child share certain learned behaviors?
- What traits might the child pass on to his or her offspring?

Accelerate Learning™

reflect •

A tiny fish called the pygmy goby lives in coral reefs. It begins its life as an egg. The goby hatches and then floats through the ocean. After about three weeks, it becomes an adult. Then, the goby lays eggs and dies. This fish only lives for about two months. A tortoise, on the other hand, lives for much longer. Tortoises hatch from eggs. Then they slowly grow into adults. Some tortoises can live for more than one hundred years!

Some animals, such as the pygmy goby, have very short life cycles. Other animals, such as the tortoise, have long life cycles. Plants have life cycles, too. They usually begin as seeds and grow into adult plants. But what exactly is a life cycle? Do all life cycles involve the same stages? Do they all happen the same way?

What happens in the life cycle of a butterfly and a beetle?

mammal: an animal that has hair or fur, is warm-blooded, and feeds milk to its young

A *life cycle* is the process of being born, growing into an adult, and dying. Life cycles of different organisms have different stages, though. For example, when a baby fox is born, it looks just like its parents, only smaller. It has four legs, big ears, and red fur. Most baby **mammals** look like their parents. But most insects do not start their lives looking like their parents. They start out looking very different from adults. Butterflies and beetles are two examples of this kind of insect.

• **Butterfly life cycle:** The egg is the first part of the butterfly life cycle. When an egg hatches, a larva comes out. A *larva* is the second part of the butterfly's life cycle. The larva does not look anything like the adult. A butterfly larva is called a caterpillar. The caterpillar eats as many leaves as it can. It grows bigger and bigger. Soon, it becomes a pupa. A pupa is the third part of the butterfly life cycle. The pupa is in a protective case. A butterfly pupa is called a chrysalis. Inside the chrysalis, the pupa turns into an adult butterfly. When the chrysalis cracks open, an adult butterfly comes out. The adult butterfly looks very different from the caterpillar. The adult lives for several weeks, lays eggs, and then dies.

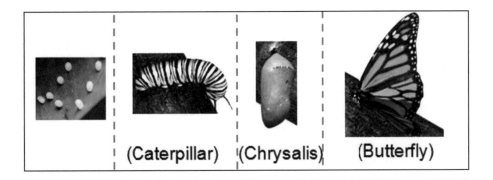

(Caterpillar)　(Chrysalis)　(Butterfly)

Accelerate Learning™

- **Beetle life cycle:** The beetle life cycle is similar to the butterfly life cycle. It also has four parts. The beetle starts out as an egg. The egg hatches and a tiny larva comes out. The larva looks like a worm and is called a mealworm. The mealworm eats as much as it can and grows larger. Then it starts the pupa part of its life cycle. It wraps itself up in a protective case. Soon, an adult beetle comes out of the pupa case. The adult beetle looks very different from the mealworm. The adult beetle may live for several weeks or months. It will lay eggs and then die.

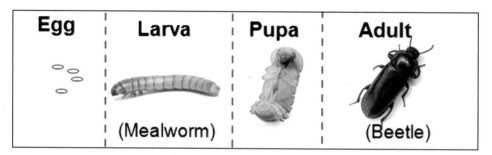

Egg	Larva	Pupa	Adult
	(Mealworm)		(Beetle)

look out!

Most insects have a life cycle with four parts. But some insects have a life cycle with only three parts. A grasshopper is an example of an insect with three parts in its life cycle. A grasshopper starts as an egg. When the egg hatches, a small version of an adult grasshopper comes out. This small version is called a *nymph*. It grows and eventually turns into an adult. It looks similar to the adult grasshopper but doesn't have full wings. Once the nymph develops those full wings, we consider it an adult grasshopper and no longer a nymph.

what do you think?

How are the life cycles of the butterfly and the beetle similar? How are they different? Describe as many similarities and differences as you can.

Everyday Life: What are the parts of the human life cycle?
When you were born, you were very tiny. Most newborn babies only weigh about eight or nine pounds. A full-grown adult usually weighs about 170 pounds. That's a pretty big change!

Humans go through the same general stages of a life cycle. Life begins with the birth of a baby. Babies cannot do much on their own, but they grow quickly. Soon, they become children. Children are larger than babies. They can walk, talk, play sports, and learn more complicated things. When children turn 13, they are called teenagers. The teenage years are when the human body changes from a child to an adult. It takes several years for teenagers to develop into adults. Adults may start families and

Accelerate
Learning™

have children of their own. When adults get very old, their bodies begin to weaken. Many activities like walking and exercising are more difficult than they were when they were younger adults. Older adults continue aging until they die.

What happens in the life cycle of a radish plant and a lima bean plant?
Plants begin their lives as seeds. They grow into small plants. Eventually, they become adult plants. Unlike insects, young plants look a lot like adult plants. Let's learn more about the life cycles of two types of plants.

• **Radish:** Radishes are a delicious plant that humans can eat. The seed part of the radish life cycle is very short. Once a radish seed is planted, it grows into a seedling in about three or four days. A *seedling*, or sprout, is a young plant that grows out of the seed. It is much smaller than the adult plant but looks pretty similar. The seedling grows for several weeks before becoming an adult plant. The adult radish plant grows flowers. These flowers turn into seeds. The seeds fall onto the ground and may begin to grow into new radish plants.

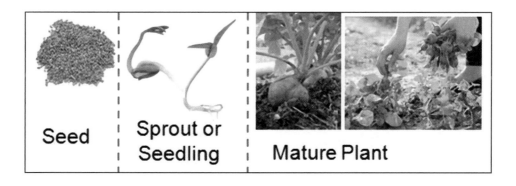

• **Lima Bean:** Have you ever eaten lima beans? Cooked lima beans are a nutritious part of a meal. A lima bean plant also starts as a seed. The seed is inside the bean. When the lima bean is watered, the bean swells. The sides of the bean break and the seeds spill out. Once planted, a seedling grows out of the seed after about seven days. A lima bean plant grows into an adult in a few months. The adult plant grows beans. When the seeds inside the beans fall to the ground, new lima bean plants might start to grow.

Accelerate Learning™

LIFE CYCLES

To learn more about a bean plant's life cycle, grow your own bean plants.

1. You will need a few different kinds of dried beans. Lima, kidney beans, and green beans work well. Do not eat any uncooked beans. They can make you sick.

2. Soak the beans in cool water overnight. Be sure to soak them in separate containers so you do not mix the different bean types.

3. Put four or five of each type of bean in their own plastic, zippered baggie. Place moist paper towels or cotton balls in with the beans. Put the plastic bags in a warm place. The bags do not need to be in sunlight.

4. Check the bags each day for several days. Write down your observations.

5. How many days did it take for the first seedling to appear? Which type of bean sprouted first? Which type sprouted last? What do the seedlings look like?

6. Find images of what each adult bean plant looks like. Do the seedlings look similar to the adult plants? Do they look different?

What Do You Know?

Look at the chart below. It contains lists of words that are related to life cycles. Each list has one word that does not belong. Circle the word that does not belong. Use the space in the right column to explain why it does not belong.

Which item does not belong?	Why doesn't this item belong?
Chrysalis Adult beetle Caterpillar	
Sprout Seed Larva	
Mealworm Pupa Caterpillar	

Acting Out an Insect Life Cycle

Help your child explore the life cycle of an insect by engaging in some dramatic play.

1. Work with your child to research the life cycle of an insect (other than a butterfly or beetle) that undergoes complete metamorphosis, such as a honeybee. Discuss with your child that complete metamorphosis has four stages: egg, pupa, larva, and adult. Incomplete metamorphosis involves three stages: egg, nymph, and adult.

2. Research information about the four different stages of your insect's life cycle. Try to find out where the adults lay their eggs and what the larva eats. Read about the pupa stage and learn about any special names for the protective case. Find out what the adult insect looks like and describe how it is different from the larva. Try to find images of all four stages of this insect's life cycle.

3. When you have collected all of this information, work with your child to create a skit or puppet show about your insect's life cycle. Your child could dress up as the insect in each of the four stages. You could also construct puppets from felt or construction paper and put on a puppet show.

Here are some questions to discuss with students:

- What does the larva stage of this insect look like? What does the adult stage look like?

- Do the larva and adult look similar?

- How long is this insect's life cycle? How much time does each stage of the life cycle last?

GLOSSARY OF TERMS

Adaptation – An inherited trait or learned behavior that helps an organism survive in its surroundings

Adaptation – Any characteristic that helps a plant or animal survive

Camouflage – Characteristics that blend in with the surrounding environment and increase chances of survival

Carnivore – An animal that gets energy by eating only other animals

Change – Become different

Characteristics – Traits or features that cannot be changed

Classify – Group together based on similar traits

Clay – A component of soil that is usually a red-orange color; texture is thick and sticky when wet

Closed circuit – A pathway that allows an electric current to flow freely

Cold front – The location where a cold air mass is replacing a warm air mass

Condensation – Physical change in matter from a gas to a liquid

Condensation – The changing of gaseous water vapor in the air to liquid water

Conductor – Material that allows electric current to flow through easily

Conservation – Protection and avoiding wasteful and destructive use

Consumer – An organism that gets energy from eating other organisms

Deposition – The build up of land by the settlement of sediment and soil in a new location

Development – Growth

Dissolve – To breakdown and spread out evenly in a liquid

Ecosystem – A community of living and nonliving things in their natural environment

Electric current – The flow of electricity through a circuit

Electrical circuit – The pathway through which electrical current flows

Electrical energy – Energy produced by a power source

Electricity – Energy created by the movement of electrons

Electromagnetic field – A magnetic field created by an electrical current

Energy – What is needed to do work or cause change

GLOSSARY OF TERMS

Environment – The living and nonliving things that are around an organism

Erosion – Wearing away of Earth's surface by wind, water, or ice

Evaporation – The changing of water from liquid to a gas

Float – Stay on the surface level in a liquid

Food web – A connection of food chains with many food energy paths in an ecosystem

Force – A push or pull that causes an object to move, stop, or change direction

Friction – A force that slows or stops motion when objects rub together

Generation – The lifespan of an organism

Glacier – A large, slow-moving, long-lasting accumulation of snow and ice that develops on land

Gravel – A component of soil made of small pieces of rock; pebbles; usually a smooth texture

Gravity – The force that pulls objects toward the center of Earth

Herbivore – An animal that gets energy by eating only plants

Inherited – Passed from parent to offspring during reproduction

Insulator – Material that prevents electric current or heat from flowing

Learned behavior – A change in a way an animal acts as a result of its experience

Life cycle – The stages in an organism's life from birth to death

Light Energy – Energy that can be seen by the eye

Liquid – Substance that takes the shape of its container and flows

Magnetism – The property of attraction to a magnet

Magnetism – The pushing or pulling force produced by a magnet

Mass – The amount of stuff in something, measured in kg

Matter – Anything that has mass and takes up space

Mechanical energy – Energy produced by a machine or moving part

Melt – Change in matter from a solid to a liquid

Mix – To combine together

Mixture – A combination of two or more substances where each keep their own properties and can be easily separated

GLOSSARY OF TERMS

Moon – A natural satellite that orbits a planet

Moon phase – What the moon looks like at different times of the month

Movement – A change in position of location

Nonrenewable resource – A resource that nature cannot replace

Offspring – The child or offshoot from a parent

Omnivore – An animal that gets energy by eating both plants and other animals

Open circuit – A pathway that prevents electric current from flowing freely or stops the flow

Pattern – A design that is repeated

Photosynthesis – The process where plants use sunlight, water, and carbon dioxide to produce sugar and release oxygen

Physical properties – The look, feel, taste, sound, or smell of an object

Physical states of matter – Solid, liquid, gas

Position – Where an object is located

Precipitation – Rain, snow, sleet, or hail that falls from clouds in the sky

Predator – An organism that hunts and feeds on another animal

Prey – An animal that is hunted as food

Producer – An organism that uses sunlight to make its own food for energy

Pull – Use force to move towards

Push – Use force to move away

Rain gauge – A tool that measures amount of rain

Renewable resource – A resource that nature can replace

Reproduction – The act of making something new

Retain – To hold inside, as soil does with water

Sand – A component of soil made by the weathering of rocks into tiny grains; rough and gritty texture

Sediment – Small pieces of rock broken down by weathering and then settling in an area

Separate – Divide or keep apart

Shadow – An area without light

Sink – Drop below the surface level in a liquid

Soil – Mixture of sand, silt, clay, rock and humus (plant and animal remains)

GLOSSARY OF TERMS

Solid – An object with a set volume and shape

Solution – A special mixture where two or more substances combine evenly

Sound energy – Energy produced from vibration that you can hear

Sun – The star at the center of the Solar System that supplies heat and light to Earth

Thermal/heat energy – Energy that causes a change in temperature between materials

Thermometer – A tool that measures temperature

Tide – The rise and fall of the water in the ocean

Topsoil – The top layer of soil; a mixture of types of Earth; texture will vary

Trait – An internal or external characteristic or feature

Warm front – The location where a warm air mass is replacing a cooler air mass

Water cycle – The changes to water as it moves up in the air and then back down to Earth's surface

Weather – The current condition of the air outdoors such as temperature, cloud cover, wind speed, and rainfall

Weathering – The breakdown of rock into smaller particles from the effects of wind, water, and ice

Wind vane – A tool that shows wind direction

NOTES

NOTES

NOTES

NOTES